Taunton's

ALL NEW

Built-Ins
IDEA BOOK

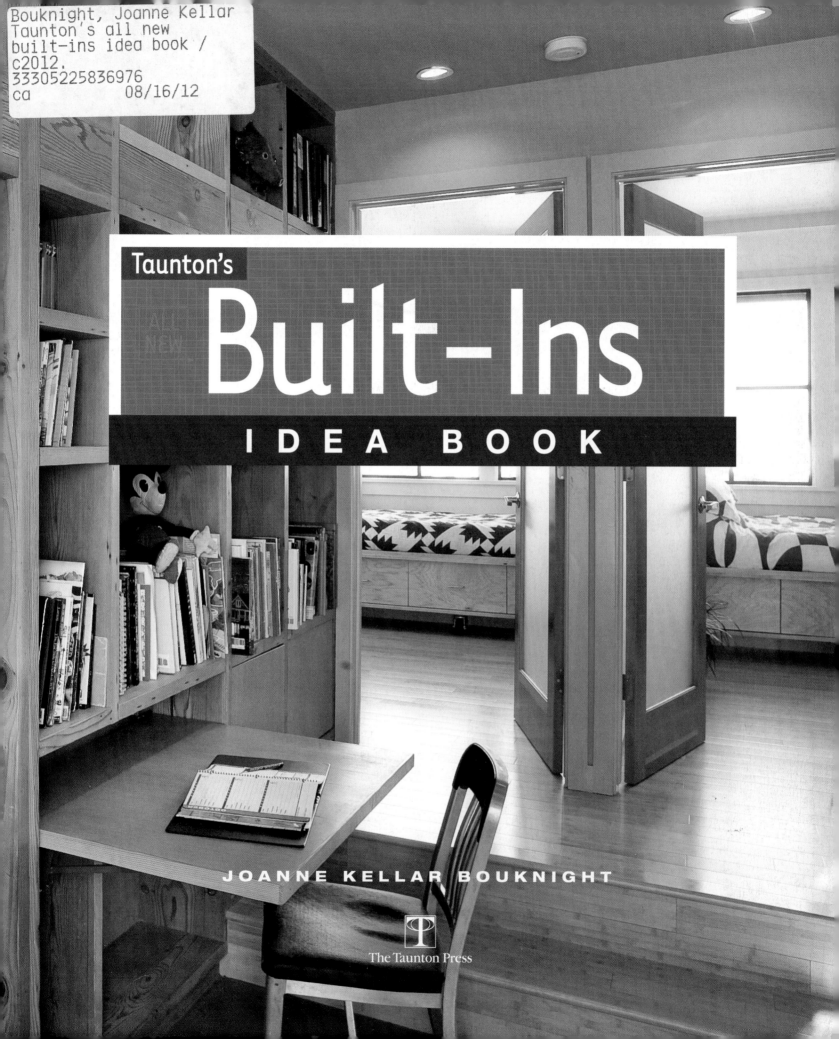

Taunton's

ALL NEW

Built-Ins

IDEA BOOK

JOANNE KELLAR BOUKNIGHT

The Taunton Press

To The Taunton Press, for the chance to be part of their homebuilding community.

Text © 2012 by Joanne Kellar Bouknight
Illustrations © 2012 by The Taunton Press, Inc.

The Taunton Press
Inspiration for hands-on living®

The Taunton Press, Inc., 63 South Main Street, PO Box 5506, Newtown, CT 06470-5506
e-mail: tp@taunton.com

Editor: Alex Giannini
Copy editor: Seth Reichgott
Jacket/Cover design: Kimberly Adis
Interior design: Kimberly Adis
Layout: Laura Lind Design
Illustrator: Joanne Kellar Bouknight
Cover Photographers: (Front cover): Eric Roth; (Back cover, clockwise from top): Mick Hales; Mick Hales;
Charles Miller, courtesy of *Fine Homebuilding* © The Taunton Press; Eric Roth

Fine Homebuilding® is a trademark of The Taunton Press, Inc., registered in the U.S. Patent and Trademark Office.

The following names/manufacturers appearing in *Taunton's All New Built-Ins Idea Book* are trademarks: IKEA®,
The National Kitchen and Bath Association®, EnergyStar®, Häfele®, Homasote®

Library of Congress Cataloging-in-Publication Data
Bouknight, Joanne Kellar.
  Taunton's all new built-ins idea book / Joanne Kellar Bouknight.
     p. cm.
  Includes bibliographical references and index.
  ISBN 978-1-60085-388-3 (alk. paper)
  1. Built-in furniture--Design and construction. 2. Cabinetwork. 3. Storage in the home. I. Title.
  TT197.5.B8B68 2012
  645'.4--dc23
                              2011031735

Printed in the United States of America
10 9 8 7 6 5 4 3 2 1

acknowledgments

tHIS BOOK IS THE BRAINCHILD OF PETER CHAPMAN, Executive Editor of homebuilding, home design and woodworking books, who figured it was time to refocus on one of the most comforting aspects of a home, its built-ins. Thanks, Peter!

Just as it's tough to name all the people who take a house from dream to reality, it's impossible to list everyone who's had a hand on the built-ins in this book. Thanks to you all! I am grateful to the homeowners who offered their homes and time for our photo shoots. My thanks to our photo shoot photographers, Mick Hales, Lincoln Barbour, and Eric Roth. And many thanks to the photographers who shot many of the remaining built-ins in this book: Ryann Ford, Hulya Kolabas, Eric Roth, Susan Teare, and Brian Vanden Brink. But there are more: Please refer to the credits in the back of the book for names of photographers for individual photos; please accept my apology for any omissions.

My thanks to the many designers and architects whose work is in this book, and especially to the following, who designed many of these built-ins and who took extra time and energy to give me detailed information about their work: Albertsson Hansen Architects, Arkin Tilt Architects, Bonaventura Architects, CAST Architecture, CWB (Coburn Welch Boutin) Architects, eM/Zed design architecture & planning, Laura Kaehler Architects, Lynn Hopkins Architect, Pill Maharam Architects, Rehkamp Larson Architects, Samsel Architects, Silver Maple Construction, and ZeroEnergy Design. And please refer to the back of this book for a list of designers with multiple projects, and to the photo credits for individual designer names; again, my apologies if I've left out anyone.

The driving force behind this book is, of course, The Taunton Press, which for years has been both a source of inspiration and an incomparable resource for the design, construction, and ownership of houses. Thanks to Taunton Books for their patience, trust, persistence, and foresight. There's Peter Chapman; he's at the top of this page and my list. My day-to-day thanks go to my editor, the thorough, thoughtful (and quick!), and upbeat Alex Giannini, and to Taunton Books' photo editor, the organized, perceptive, and multi-talented Katy Binder. Thanks to art director Alison Wilkes, for giving me the opportunity to do the drawings start to finish, and to Sandy Mahlstedt. Thanks again to *Fine Homebuilding* for their homebuilding genius. Specific thanks to Chuck Miller for letting me mine for photos and to Brian Pontolilo and Chuck Bickford and all the editors past and present for their dedication and expertise.

As with my other books and with every aspect of my life 24/7, I thank my colleagues around town for their patience, and I am grateful to my friends and my family both near and far for their support. As ever, my abiding gratitude to Neil, who works harder than anyone I know but always has time to give me architectural advice and moral support, and to our sons Sebastian and Cornelius, who had the wisdom to be away at college during most of my book-making time.

contents

introduction   2

why built-ins?   4

cabinets, drawers, and shelves   12

seating   38

entryways, hallways, and stairways   50

kitchens and dining   68

6

**living
spaces**   94

7

workspaces   114

8

**bedrooms
and closets**   126

9

bathrooms   146

resources   166

designers   167

photo credits   168

introduction

N MY BOOK, A BUILT-IN is a nailed-down element that goes beyond the basic house container, with the express purpose of making a house more functional and livable and, especially, more personal, more comfortable, more home.

Finish trim details, such as crown molding and wainscoting, are certainly built-in and go beyond the basic framework of the house. Likewise, built-out structures such as soffits or furred-out columns can add stability and containment to a space. This book is filled with beautiful examples of these architectural elements, but the text focuses primarily on built-ins that hold things, built-ins that are workhorses for a home: cabinets, shelves, seats, fireplace surrounds, closets.

The book begins with an in-depth look at the basic components of built-ins. The following chapters take a tour through the house, starting at the front door and working inward, to the kitchen, living spaces, workspaces, bedrooms, and bathrooms. Ending the book are resources for further reading and a list of architects and designers who have multiple projects in this book.

As you research built-ins beyond this book, do some seat-of-the-pants investigation, literally. When you come across a built-in that feels just right to you, like a breakfast booth in a friend's house, take note of why you like it. Write down why and take photos. It never hurts to pack a small tape measure in your bag for such occasions. How deep is that built-in seat? How high? Is the back slanted? Is the ceiling lowered over the breakfast nook?

Where to put built-ins? Anywhere you can! Claim potentially lost space: the kneewall under a sloped ceiling, the stud wall for shallow shelves. Fit drawers and closets under stairs, if legal, or tuck them under built-in seating. Add a super-shallow hutch to a kitchen hallway. Make built-ins easy to use: place prime storage between 20 in. and

40 in. above the floor. Keep shelves shallow so that it is easy to see everything. If storage must be deep, choose either a pull-out shelf behind a door or a drawer. Both of these options are easier to access than deep shelves behind doors. Use full-extension drawers. Wire pulls and levers are easier to pull than small knobs. If you are renovating, as you home in on the built-ins you really want, mark out their potential locations on the floor with blue painter's tape—the kind that peels off easily. Built-ins can fill in a space that's too big or smooth out irregular corners.

If you've got built-in cabinets or book-shelves that are functional but tired looking, consider simple uplifts. New paint colors, especially, can transform. Paint insides of open shelves a deeper color to make contents pop visually. Paint shelf edges or add a decorative trim. Well-built cabinets that are still sturdy but tired looking can be refaced or even given new doors. Revive base cabinet

interiors with roll-out shelves to make it easier to grab pots and pans.

As you consider built-ins, it makes economic and common sense to look for ways to save energy and resources, and to make it easier to live comfortably. Choose EnergyStar® appliances for kitchens and laundry rooms, look for low-voltage or lower-energy fixtures, choose cabinetry with no or low formaldehyde content, and select low-VOC finishes for cabinetry. If you are building from scratch and are still in the idea-gathering stage, one of the most significant steps you can take to save energy and boost comfort is to swap out some square footage for built-in cubic footage. You may find that a smaller kitchen with well-placed built-ins can be more functional and comfortable than a great big kitchen.

why built-ins?

● ● ●

YOU CAN'T OVERESTIMATE THE VALUE THAT BUILT-INS ADD TO A house. Certainly a house will cost more to build when you add more elements to its bare bones. So why use built-ins at all? Todd Hansen and Christine Albertsson of Albertsson Hansen Architects in Minneapolis, who designed the coat closet on the facing page, answer that question with this description of how built-ins simply make life easier:

"We like to add the word 'well' to 20th-century architect Le Corbusier's famous statement so that it reads, 'A house is a machine for living *well* in.' We think of rooms not merely as linked boxes with holes in them with furniture and casework lined up against the walls, but rather as spaces that are surrounded with the equipment for living well. When you reach out in a well-designed house, a cabinet or shelf is there to hold the materials for that life activity, be it a built-in buffet, a window seat, built-in bookshelves, or even an entire storage room hidden behind a cabinet door. The goal is to have the equipment and material support for living well readily at hand. With this approach, the cabinetry and other built-ins become an integral part of the architecture itself. Walls are thickened where needed to accommodate storage and display for the stuff of everyday life. A built-in banquette with lift-up seats becomes furniture as well as storage. The configuration and design of these elements becomes a significant part of the character and expression of the interior of a house, and when successful, contributes to the ability to live well in a home."

This bright walk-in coat closet with smart and understated built-ins is part of an addition to an early-20th-century Tudor house.

built-ins
define style
and shape
space

●●● BUILT-INS CAN DEFINE A ROOM'S STYLE with details, color, shape, size, and configuration. Design built-ins in harmony with the existing style of your home by incorporating the same trim or proportions, or take the opposite tack and design new built-ins in a contrasting style, such as modern cabinets in a traditional home. Either way, make the design purposeful, not a near miss. Built-ins can shape a room physically. While built-in cabinets, bookshelves, and seating will give character and a sense of shelter to any space, they are particularly valuable for making a too-big and characterless space more comfortable. A bank of cabinets can carve a room into smaller, more intimate spaces and can guide circulation. Tall bookshelves can create a visual buffer so that a private space is sheltered from a public space. But built-ins are a boon for small spaces, too, as they can add tidy storage from floor to ceiling, even when tucked into a stud wall.

This deep, snug-as-a-bug bedroom window-sill/seat is the inspired result of transforming a gristmill office building into a house. A concrete storage bunker within the building was turned into a bedroom by covering the interior walls with narrow spruce boards, salvaged from grist-mill bins, and by fitting the opening with operable double-hung windows and a wood sill.

ABOVE Cheery enough to spend time in, this hallway is packed full of closets, both tall and small. The tall doors stop short of the baseboard to look more like lockers and to keep contents from spilling out.

ABOVE The most magical of built-ins is a secret door to a secret room. Shelves on the door help disguise the door's function and become accessible from the sitting room when the door is open.

A clear view from the second floor offers a glimpse of the floor-to-ceiling maple cabinetry in the living room. Shelves hold electronic equipment, a sculpture collection, and an abundance of books. Closed-door cabinets hold more media.

built-ins make storage and display space

●●● BUILT-IN CABINETS AND CLOSETS ARE, OF course, highly functional, and that's a perfect reason to build them in anywhere you see fit. Cabinets and closets store your gear so it doesn't look cluttered and so that you can retrieve it when you need it. Built-in shelves offer display space for your treasures, from collections and art objects to photographs and books. You can choose open shelves or closed, depending on your needs and how much dusting is tolerable. Pocket doors can be a compromise between being either open all the time or closed all the time. Shelves can be adjustable, especially for kids, but keep them fixed if you know what you'll be storing and don't plan on moving shelves around. When versatility is prime or space is at a premium, however, sometimes it's best to stick to furniture rather than built-ins, such as using a rolling cart instead of an island in a small kitchen.

BELOW This built-in cabinet turns a potentially awkward junction between sloped ceiling and countertop into good-looking storage for toiletries, complete with a sweet cubby for a box of tissues.

A kitchen for a working farm was renovated to create more space, with a butcher-block island that doubles as space for five to eat or for two to prepare dinner. The hutch at left has a flip-down door that becomes a desk; the house phone is inside the niche. Cantilevered shelves on the back wall are supported on brackets.

ABOVE Built-in sliding-door closets not only conceal plenty of storage space but offer space for kids to draw and parents to write to-do lists and tack up notes.

RIGHT These captivating shelves are both semi-recessed and projecting, allowing books to sit within the shelve niches and on top.

RIGHT Symmetry and informality make this entryway built-in both relaxing and cheerful. Three simple boxes are divided into cubbies with fixed shelves, while the upper boxes are fitted with hooks supported on boards for coats and sports gear.

built-ins add comfort and charm

● ● ● THE SPACE- AND STYLE-SHAPING QUALITIES of built-ins, along with obvious utility, are what add security, appeal, and comfort to a room as well as to a home. A built-in breakfast nook can bring the busy members of a family together in close quarters for at least a little while, either at breakfast or during an informal dinner. People are by nature drawn to light, so a built-in window seat makes a favorite destination. Bookshelves on each side and a lowered ceiling above can create a cozy niche for a solo person to read a book or watch the skies or for several people to snuggle and have a

ABOVE There's a sneak peek into the kitchen from this entryway bench, and wood paneling and an operable window bring the look of the outdoors inside. At right is a full-height built-in coat cabinet.

RIGHT Lowering the ceiling over a built-in seat increases the sense of enclosure and security and makes a nice contrast to the distant view. Double rows of drawers make good use of the space beneath the seat.

A gas fireplace next to a built-in soaking tub offers the ultimate in comfort. A deep recess with clear finished shelves and sides offers easy-to-reach storage for towels.

ABOVE This serene entry bench is supported by walls for a streamlined look. Storage for coats and boots is concealed in the closet at right.

RIGHT For extra charm and coziness, the niche is framed, trimmed, and fitted with a small window to the hall. Generous storage drawers fill in under the seating.

cabinets, drawers, and shelves

● ● ●

IT'S HARD TO IMAGINE A HOUSE WITHOUT THE MOST BASIC AND ubiquitous of built-ins: cabinets, drawers, and shelves. Kitchens and bathrooms are obvious spaces for built-in cabinets, but cabinets can help organize and beautify any room. Consider media cabinetry for living and entertainment spaces, cabinets for computers and their peripherals in workspaces, and built-ins for storing clothes, linens, and toys in bedrooms and closets.

Cabinets are meant to be functional workhorses, but they also set the style, and their bulk has a big impact on traffic patterns. So dedicate plenty of time to select and position these essential—and potentially pricey—built-ins. Compare cabinet sources and cabinet materials and think outside the box when it comes to configuration. For example, do you really want to load an outside wall with both base and wall cabinets when there's the potential for a great view? Built-in cabinets can make more of an impact when they're used judiciously, so don't pack every square inch.

Although the cabinet is the king of storage built-ins, the open shelf can be both the most basic and the most showy of built-ins. That simple horizontal surface has so many possibilities. A shelf can go in any room, anywhere, and be any size, from the spice-jar shelf tucked into a stud space to a substantial fireplace mantel wide enough to display art or pottery. For shelves that will hold heavy loads, such as books, you'll want to consider materials and dimensions carefully.

A well-fit butler's pantry mixes traditional and modern details. Furniture-like cabinet feet, reclaimed Southern yellow pine flooring, oiled and waxed southern yellow pine countertops, tongue-and-groove paneling, and a hefty apron sink convey the look of an early-20th-century country house. Ideal for reaching top shelves in this 9-ft.-high space, the ladder can be rolled from the pantry into the kitchen.

cabinets

●●● EACH PART OF A CABINET CONTRIBUTES to its style and function. First, there's the case type—that's the basic box—and next are the door and drawer types, along with cabinet finishes, cabinet part configuration, and hardware. The two basic types of cabinets are face frame and frameless (see the sidebar on the facing page), whereas doors and drawers can be inset or overlay and can be configured as solid slabs or with panels and trim (see the drawing on p. 23). Frameless, or Euro-style, cabinets have long been used in modern or contemporary style rooms; they can be beefed up with moldings and panels to look traditional. And the more traditional face-frame cabinets can look streamlined, depending on the door type. But feel free to mix up hardware and cabinet styles for a lively interaction, if that's your fancy. For example, fanciful sculptural pulls can spice up traditional cabinets, and, on the flip side, high-quality classic hardware can add gravitas to stock cabinets.

ABOVE A home office features a wall of built-ins, with full-overlay thumb-pull drawers across the lower third and a mix of fixed and adjustable open shelves above. The highlight of the built-in is a well-lit glazed display case that showcases a model of a famous U.S. whaler.

BELOW For the most streamlined of frameless cabinets, these full-overlay one-piece doors and drawer are operated by touch hardware.

WHAT'S THE DIFFERENCE BETWEEN FACE-FRAME AND FRAMELESS CABINETS?

THE CABINET CASE

- The face frame can make it easier to fit cabinets into a space that isn't completely square and plumb.
- A face-frame cabinet has a narrower opening than a frameless cabinet of the same width, so pull-out shelves and drawers must be narrower.
- A frameless cabinet has no stile or rail in front of contents, so it can be easier to pull out stored items.
- A face-frame cabinet gets much of its strength from the face frame, whereas a frameless cabinet depends on a stronger, thicker back and strong corner joints.

DOORS AND DRAWERS

- In frameless cabinets, doors and drawers usually overlay the case completely (these are called full overlay, or flush overlay); frameless cabinets occasionally have inset doors.
- In face-frame cabinets, doors and drawers may overlay the frame completely, but they are more likely to be inset or to overlay the frame partially (reveal overlay or half overlay).
- Inset doors, which are the traditional standard in Colonial and Shaker-style cabinets, require more precision in their making and installation.

DOOR HARDWARE

- Concealed adjustable hinges are available for both frameless and face-frame cabinet doors. They commonly adjust in three directions and are easy to adjust over the lifetime of the cabinet.
- Inset doors traditionally are hung with butt hinges, which require more precision to install than adjustable hinges. A butt hinge, and its close cousin, the olive-knuckle hinge, are likely the hinge of choice on glass-door cabinets, as the concealed adjustable hinge would no longer be concealed.

CABINET SHELVES

- Fixed or adjustable shelves can be a less expensive option in both frameless and face-frame cabinets than pull-out shelves, which require slide hardware.
- Pull-out shelves offer easier overall access to contents than fixed and adjustable shelves.

Face-frame cabinet

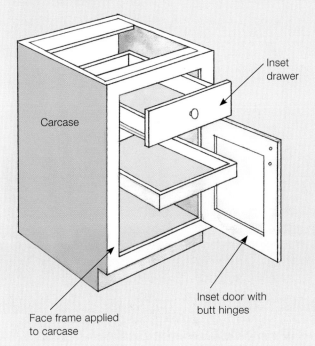

Carcase

Inset drawer

Face frame applied to carcase

Inset door with butt hinges

Frameless cabinet

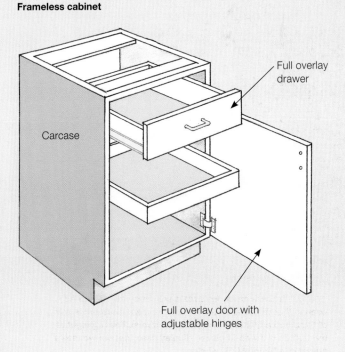

Carcase

Full overlay drawer

Full overlay door with adjustable hinges

WHAT'S IN A CABINET CASE?

p articleboard is the least expensive and lowest quality of case goods and is the most commonly used case material in manufactured cabinets. There's not a clear consensus about what makes the best cabinet case. For years, the highest-quality wood-based cabinet cases have been made from ¾-in. veneer-core plywood, which is stronger, lighter, more resistant to moisture, and better at taking fasteners than medium-density fiberboard or particleboard. Although MDF is heavier and more vulnerable to water damage than veneer-core plywood, it is less expensive and it has dimensional stability and a smooth face, ideal for applying veneers and laminates. If your budget allows, choose plywood for cabinets where water could potentially cause damage. But for dry locations, also consider the recent plywood mashup, combi-core. Combi-core plywood retains the strong and light veneer plywood core but is sandwiched between layers of MDF to provide a smooth, stable surface.

The interior of a case can be painted, veneered with plastic laminate or wood, or finished more economically with vinyl, foil, or paper films. Melamine fused to particleboard is a less expensive and easy-to-clean alternative and requires no finishing on site. Most wood or wood-veneered cabinets are finished in the shop, or at least primed if they are paint grade.

If you are concerned about chemical sensitivity, it's good to know that plywood, MDF, and particle-board typically emit less formaldehyde than in the past because of improved glues. Although formaldehyde levels are very low in all these products, veneer-core plywood contains the least, whereas MDF has more than particleboard. Also look for cabinets with "no-added formaldehyde" or consider all-metal cabinets, but be prepared for higher prices.

Choose a cabinet case with a back—¼ in. thick minimum or ½ in. for extra strength—for strength, stiffness, and to prevent objects from slipping out of the back of the cabinet.

A generous built-in bench stretches the length of this airy kitchen to create a cozy space for reading or chatting with the cook. Deep window aprons make room for bowls. Cabinets are face-frame, with inset doors and drawers.

White frameless cabinets with full-overlay doors and drawers add an almost seamless impression to this bright kitchen.

This graceful maple cabinet is a hybrid variety, with a frameless case that is trimmed only around the outer edges with a 1½-in. surround. Frameless cases are usually finished off with overlay doors and drawers, but these are inset from the surround. Two horizontal rails in the glass doors offset each other to add a subtle balance to the symmetry (you can see the right rail, but the left rail is behind the pendant light fixture).

•cabinet configurations

Cabinet dimensions vary depending on their use and on standard ergonomic considerations. For specific size suggestions, see the chapters on built-ins for each room in the house. You can customize cabinet heights, depths, and layout if you order semi-custom or custom cabinets, or if you have the know-how to retrofit knock-down (KD) or ready-to-assemble (RTA) cabinets. Although taller cabinets can be a back saver for tall people, think carefully about choosing an unconventional height for all cabinets in a kitchen or bathroom, as it may not appeal to buyers in the future. But if you plan on staying in your house a long time, go ahead and build to suit.

Kitchen and bathroom cabinetry, and some cabinetry in other rooms, features a toespace, or a toekick. Created by the recessed frame that supports the cabinet or from trim that conceals cabinet support legs, the standard toespace is 4 in. high and 3 in. deep, whereas a European-style cabinet often sports a toespace from 5 in. to 8 in. high. A higher toespace creates a more generous place to stand, makes it a bit easier to reach items on the bottom of the cabinet, and is more forgiving to vacuum cleaning and mopping, but also results in some lost storage space. But a higher toespace does make it easier to install a built-in step stool or heat and return-air registers. No matter how streamlined it looks, avoid a toespace lower than 4 in., as it will be tough to clean well.

Unfitted-style cabinetry features a dark-painted toespace flanked with legs that mimic the look of furniture. Pilasters can be applied to corners or spaces between cabinets to add substance. In some kitchen and bath

cabinetry, cabinets are set on plinths that project from the case. This makes for an authentically traditional look, but also requires a deeply overhanging countertop to make room for your feet. A plinth or projecting base works fine for cabinetry in a living room or study, as you aren't working at a countertop. For cabinetry that truly looks built-in, continue the style and height of the wall base around the cabinetry. If you prefer to finish off a built-in bookcase or cabinet with the look of furniture, consider a base shape and size that differs from the baseboard.

Open shelves mix with closed cabinetry to add depth, texture, and color to a hallway study. Cabinet doors are traditional inset frame-and-flat-panel doors, echoing the frame-and-panel design of the paneling. These cabinets have bases aligned with the face frames and trimmed with baseboard.

LEFT The old-world feel of this kitchen comes in large part from the warm, furniture-like cabinetry, with curved legs at the corner and the massive curved natural wood apron.

BELOW Mahogany frame-and-panel doors with a fine-furniture finish, brushed nickel pulls, and the dark stone backsplash and countertop give the kitchen an elegance in keeping with its increased visual connection to the rest of the house.

ABOVE These built-in cabinets support shelves, not workspaces, so bases don't require toespaces.

A built-in living room cabinet is simple and clean, with simple molding, small pulls, and a few thick, white shelves that are refreshingly uncluttered and home to just a few favorite objects.

This stack of custom-built face-frame cabinets acts like a hutch or pantry, with storage for all sizes of kitchen gear. Shallow one-piece drawers in the base cabinet handle silverware, cutlery, kitchen wraps, and linens. The middle doors flip up and slide in to access small appliances.

abinet sources range widely, and, in fact, cabinet components themselves are likely to come from various sources. Even custom cabinetmakers may shop out components to specialized sources, then assemble the components in their own shops. Stock and semi-custom cabinets increasingly come from one of the many cabinet manufacturers that purchase cabinet parts from companies that specialize in doors, drawers, or cases. That's not a bad thing if the components are well made and reliable.

Stock cabinets are bought off the shelf or ordered from a big-box store, home center, or lumberyard, or through a kitchen designer or contractor. Stock cabinets are built as individual cases and in standard sizes (usually 3-in. increments), and filler pieces are required to fill gaps if a stretch of cabinets is narrower than the allotted space. Semi-custom cabinets tend to be higher quality than stock and lay claim to more sizes and configurations, and stretches of cabinets can be made to order rather than purchased case by case. Custom cabinets tend to cost the most and take the most time, but not necessarily. You can often save money by purchasing off-the-shelf aftermarket innards such as dividers and knife blocks, so comparison shop before placing a cabinet order.

If you're handy, consider going the DIY route with KD or RTA cabinets (these are sometimes sold only to the trade). These cabinet parts are factory made and prefinished and are shipped to you unassembled, with all the holes drilled and the fasteners and parts required for assembly. Thinking of purchasing cabinets from the KD world leader, IKEA? Pick up cabinets at an IKEA store and you'll pay much less than if the cabinet components are shipped.

If a cabinet redo isn't in the budget, look for changes that can cost less but make a visual, and even functional, difference. Replacing door and drawer faces, which is often called refacing, can be a less expensive alternative, but make sure the cabinet cases are in good shape. Moldings can be attached to flat doors and drawer faces for a 3-D do-over. Replace fixed shelves in base cabinets with pull-out shelves. All-new pulls or knobs can completely change a cabinet's attitude, and never underestimate the punch that repainting cabinets can give to a room.

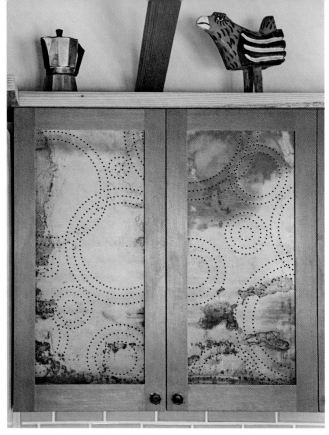

ABOVE These punched-metal door panels set in overlay wood frames are a contemporary take on the metal pie safe, a cupboard with perforated tin doors that allow air to circulate, but not insects and mice.

RIGHT In a butler's pantry, flipper doors on upper cabinets prevent head banging.

• doors and drawers

Whether inset or overlay, doors and drawers can be as streamlined or ornate as you like. The simplest of doors and drawers is a flat slab. Frame-and-panel doors can themselves be simple or complex. Panels can be flat, raised, or made of beadboard or clear, frosted, or textured glass. Because wall cabinets are the most visible, they make good candidates for more detail, and for glass panels. Clear glass is ideal for showcasing prized items, whereas textured or frosted glass can showcase a cabinet's contents in a more subtle way. Ideally, glass cabinets with prized possessions can be fit up with lighting along the top or sides.

Door frames are often made of solid wood, and panels can be as well, but the smooth surface of MDF has made it increasingly popular for doors and drawer fronts of all styles. Top-of-the-line drawers are usually built from solid hardwood sides and fronts and plywood bottoms. Doors and drawer fronts can be finished using the same methods as the insides of cabinets (see the sidebar on the facing page).

Doors and drawers should be compatible, but they don't need to match. Think paneled doors with slab (one-piece) drawers, for example. A wide but shallow drawer can look awkward if built with a frame and panel, as the panel can seem too long and thin in comparison to the frame.

BASE CABINET DRAWER AND DOOR OPTIONS

t he two basic categories of drawers and doors are frame-and-panel or flat slab (also called one-piece, but that doesn't necessarily mean monolithic). Some cabinet cases below are shown as frameless and some are face frame, but be assured that either category of door/drawer can be used in either type of cabinet case. And note that as a rule, upper drawer detailing can be simpler than that on a door or a wide drawer below, especially if the upper drawer is shallow.

Drawer in a beaded-edge frame over a beaded frame-and-raised-panel door with butt hinges

A stack of same-size flat-slab overlay drawers with finger pulls

Graduated-size drawers inset in beaded face-frame case with intermediate rails

Graduated-size drawers inset in a face frame without intermediate rails

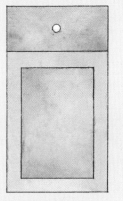

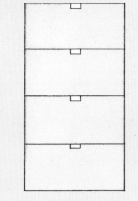
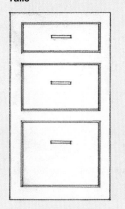

An upper shallow drawer often looks less fussy with a flat-slab drawer face.

Drawer borrows beading from the door design, but not the raised panel.

Intermediate rails provide strength and look traditional. Beading the frame instead of the drawer is a simpler, longer-lasting detail.

Eliminating intermediate rails looks less traditional but increases cabinet capacity.

Drawers and pull-out shelves with high sides make for a highly functional kitchen. These cabinets are frameless with full-overlay doors and drawers. Doors and drawers are fitted with super-wide wire pulls, which can double as towel bars if necessary.

LEFT A design goal in this renovated Victorian was to make spaces both clutter-free and kid friendly. These simple rectangular drawers fit easily into a faceted bowed window seat to make ample and functional storage for toys when playtime is over.

BELOW The three components of this elegant china and silverware cabinet are detailed to match, with a flat panel (or grille for return air, bottom) held by a frame with edge molding around its inside edges.

LEFT Fitting drawers into built-in seats is more expensive than adding top-hinged storage, but it provides tidier and much more accessible space.

DRAWER DETAILS

t oday's drawers are much wider and deeper than drawers from even two decades ago, and they're certainly much bigger than the traditional wood glide could ever hold. A wide drawer—anything over 24 in.—requires two knobs, two short pulls, or a long wire pull. Keep proportion in mind for drawer (and door) hardware: A small knob can look puny on a big drawer, and a big bin pull can look silly on a small drawer. A knob with a rose (the round plate at the base of the shaft) can keep a drawer looking neater because fingers are less likely to touch the drawer face.

For drawers that will be doing heavy lifting, holding pots, pans, dishes, heavy electronics, or file folders, look for well-built drawers with $5/8$-in. to $3/4$-in. sides of melamine, solid wood, or birch plywood. Shallow drawers can have sides as thin as $1/2$ in. Metal and plastic sides can be plenty strong and are well suited to a streamlined look. Shelves that carry heavy loads should also have thick bottoms.

Drawers are operated by slides (also called guides or glides). If possible, go for full-extension slides, which allow you to see the entire contents of a drawer. And consider quiet, self-closing slides. Most slides are side-mounted, but undermount slides, which can only be used on face-frame cabinets, create a more traditional look because they aren't exposed when the drawer is open. Undermount slides reduce the depth of a drawer, whereas side-mounted slides take a bit off the width. Those big drawers with heavy loads should be fit with glides that can carry 100 lb. or more.

Pull-out shelves, which are accessible by opening the cabinet door, are a viable alternative to full-fledged drawers, especially in base cabinets. The shelf sides are lower than a drawer's sides, affording a better look at the contents within. Pull-out shelves are suitable for taller, bulkier items in one layer, and for office equipment, such as printers, in another. Pull-out shelves operate on undermount glides.

LEFT A spice drawer near the range is in a handy location for a family that does a lot of cooking. This spice tray was designed for this particular drawer, but after-market spice-drawer accessories can do the trick, too.

RIGHT Overlay doors and drawers with matching veneer are a sophisticated, streamlined choice in this modern kitchen.

shelves

●●● A SHELF CAN BE PRACTICAL, DECORATIVE, or both at once. Open shelving makes it easier to find things and to put them back, and visibility can be an incentive to keep things tidy. On the practical side, open shelving in a walk-in pantry can make finding the fixings for dinner much faster than opening doors and searching pullout shelves. Open shelving in a kitchen can make the room seem more open and make it easier for both cook and guests to locate cooking tools and vessels. The open shelf can be a welcome addition to any room in the house where you want to display favorite collections, make it easier for family members to find things on a daily basis, or simply store stuff until you need it again. Even small items or objects that don't fit neatly on a shelf, like balls, pencils, potatoes, or candles, can fit in baskets or containers on shelves, where they're easy to see and access.

As a rule of thumb, if you are storing objects that you use often, keep the shelf almost as narrow as the objects you're storing or displaying. That way there's no possibility of stacking objects in front. This goes for every kind of shelf, from the pantry to the linen closet. In a pantry, or a large linen closet or on the space above clothes rods in closets, consider wrapping the walls—or two walls—with narrow shelves that make an L-shape or C-shape in plan rather than running wide shelves across the entire length of the space. Narrower shelves provide better visibility and easier access.

Bookshelves for kitchens, workspaces, and living rooms may differ depending on other items that are stored along with books, but here are some general guidelines for comfortable vertical clearance between shelves: 10½ in. for most books, 12 in. for magazines in stand-up storage boxes, and 13 in. to 14 in. for big art books and oversize cookbooks. Suggested bookshelf depths are between 8 in. and 12 in.

All of the shelves in this display wall are the same distance from each other, and that height is based on the size of the tallest pieces of pottery in the owners' colorful collection. Shelves are fixed to establish a regular grid and to avoid the distraction of the vertical holes required for adjustable shelves.

ABOVE Custom-built cabinets can be as shallow as you'd like. These 12-in.-deep shelves were designed for storing everything from craft supplies to books and dishware.

A bright collection of pottery and dishes deserves to be admired, so open shelving was the order here. This shelving is simply added to a face-frame cabinet case. That's wood tile in the backsplash.

ABOVE It only takes a window stool that's a few inches deeper than usual to make a shelf wide enough for plant pots. Triangular brackets support the stool.

LEFT Shelves don't necessarily require your ducks to be in a row. Containers—solid or see-through, depending on need—are perfect for corralling smaller items on shelves.

There's a niche for everything in this between-the-walls shelving at the end of a tub. Shelves and supports are equally thick, emphasizing the grid and a sense of stability.

ABOVE A cherry bookcase adds traditional coziness to a bright dining room with its tidy rows of packed-tight shelves.

RIGHT The clear cherry shelf that runs the length of this room acts as both desk and support for open shelves. Adjustable cherry shelves are trimmed with a thick edge for strength and visual heft.

FACING PAGE Shelves set into a face-frame case are trimmed with edgeband just ½ in. wider than the thickness of the shelves. This significantly strengthens the shelves and gives them a more substantial profile. Full-height pantries with super-long pulls flank these recessed shelves.

BELOW Shelves are trimmed with edgeband and supported on white metal brackets set into surface-mounted metal standards. Shelves overlap the adjacent wall to emphasize the thickness of the wall. The small metal circle on the seat contains a pull to lift a lid to a space below, where phone and cable hookups are located.

LEFT Here's a short span that only requires a skinny shelf, but fat, curved shelves of solid wood are more appealing. The shelves are supported by solid wood cleats.

ABOVE A roomful of bookcases creates a quiet space just off the master bedroom. These shelves, which are all adjustable, are trimmed with edgeband.

• shelf materials and support

Solid wood is a traditional shelf material, especially if you like natural finishes, and it's relatively strong, but solid wood can warp, and it shrinks and expands with changes in humidity. Veneered plywood makes a shelf that's more stable than solid wood and almost as strong. Its edges must be covered with a glue-on or iron-on edging or with an edge-band, which has the benefit of increasing the strength of the shelf. MDF and particleboard can't span as far as wood and plywood shelves of the same thickness and depth, but can make serviceable shelves if supports are closer together.

Here are ways to strengthen a shelf and effectively increase the load it can carry:

- Keep spans shorter. An increase in span of just 25 percent results in twice as much deflection.

- Add a cleat, a narrow board that runs continuously under the back side—of a shelf.

- Add a 1½-in. edgeband to the front or just under the front edge of the board.

- Double the thickness of the shelf by fastening two boards and finishing the front edge with a same-height band.

- Add intermediate shelf supports.

- Build a torsion box instead. This thick shelf is similar to a hollow-core door, with a honeycomb structure or plywood strips faced with two plywood skins.

Check out the Sagulator, a simple online calculator for figuring out shelf spans of various sizes and types of materials (see Resources on p. 166).

Although these open shelves screen the view from a backyard entry porch, they also allow in plenty of daylight. The thick shelves are built of two layers of MDF with a solid wood nosing and are supported by solid wood brackets.

SHELF SUPPORT OPTIONS

ADJUSTABLE SHELVES

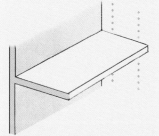

32 mm adjustable shelves

A common method of supporting shelves. Two columns of holes drilled into the sides of cabinets 32 mm apart allow a fine degree of adjustment. Shelf supports vary, from long wire clips that tuck into a groove in shelf ends to clips and pins of various shapes, sizes, and materials. The shelf in this drawing is glass for the purpose of showing the pins, but this system suits any type of shelf material.

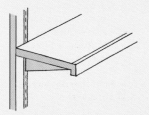

Metal standards with adjustable brackets

To add visual depth and considerable stiffness to a shelf, apply a wood edgeband (also called nosing) to the front edge.

Adjustable brackets mount into slotted standards. For a cleaner look, metal standards can be recessed into the wall.

FIXED SHELVES

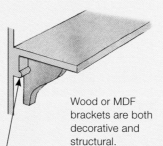

Wood or MDF brackets are both decorative and structural.

Supporting a shelf on a cleat along the back can greatly increase the load that a shelf can support or the distance it can span between brackets or wall supports.

For a truly thick shelf, apply a same-depth edgeband to a doubled layer of wood or MDF.

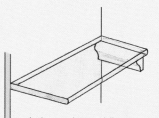

A decorative molding can act as a cleat for solid or glass shelving. A light load and/ or short span may need only supports at ends (shown), while longer spans or heavier loads may require additional support along the back.

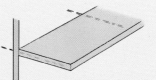

A floating shelf can be supported on hidden rods or bars that have been attached to studs. A thick floating shelf may be made of a hollow-core shelf glued to a cleat.

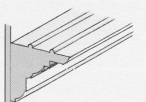

A plate rail can be built up from stock molding pieces.

A cabinet case with fixed shelves offers space for towels, beautiful objects, and toiletries at the end of this marble bath.

Adjustable shelves are aligned across the room, with the tallest shelves at the bottom for large books and stacks of magazines. Shelves are supported on metal brackets and surface-mounted standards and are trimmed with 2-in. edgeband for both stiffness and visual heft.

Maple shelves in a child's bookcase are adjustable and edgebanded. Fitting each shelf snugly against the back side of vertical stiles is extra insurance against an overloaded shelf slipping off its support pins.

more about...
FIXED OR ADJUSTABLE?

S tudies show that 99 percent of adjustable shelves are never moved. Actually, that's a made-up figure, but it's probably close to reality. Many veteran woodworkers advise that clients be discouraged from adjustable shelves, as fixed shelves are stronger and thus can have longer spans, and there's no need to drill a string of holes on each side of a cabinet or bookcase or to install metal standards. If you know you'll need adjustable shelves, say, in a child's closet, consider drilling just a few holes where you need them now and adding holes later, when it's time to move the shelf.

• build shelves into a wall

It's best to recess shelves into interior walls rather than exterior walls so as not to displace wall insulation. The exception is a knee wall or a thickened wall, which is deep enough to contain both insulation and built-in recessed shelves. Before cutting a large hole in an existing wall, make exploratory holes to determine if any utilities are running in the wall.

RIGHT Every niche in this recessed built-in shelving unit was designed for a particular piece or group of pieces in a beautiful collection of artifacts. The shelves and verticals are set back about ¼ in. to create a shadow line, and for contrast the bottom shelf has a natural stain and its rounded nosing projects past the wall.

BELOW In-wall shelves in a bedroom.

This recessed built-in shelf is detailed like the doors and window, with molding at the top, a bead running across the top of the opening, and a deep bottom shelf that looks like a window stool.

seating

● ● ●

CABINETS AND SHELVES MAY CLAIM THE PRIZE AS THE HANDIEST OF
built-ins, but built-in seating warms our hearts, along with the rest of us. We're
drawn to a built-in breakfast nook the same way we are to a booth in a restaurant,
as a cozy invitation to stuff in one more person. And built-in seating is ideal for
corralling the littlest kids, making them feel snug. While built-in seating may give you
the warm fuzzies, it can be a visual treat, too. Aesthetically, built-in seats can help
shape a room. Because it is low, broad, and deep, a window seat, breakfast booth,
or entryway bench acts as a strong and appealing visual ballast without blocking the
view between rooms or to the outdoors.

Functionally, the built-in seat is a fixed-in-place reminder that even the busiest
of us needs to sit on occasion—to put on or take off boots at the door, to enjoy
watching the snowfall from the living room, to chat with friends or family in a cozy
setting, or even to work in a location that's not quite as formal as a home office.
A built-in seat has a natural space for handling additional storage, too, if you're
careful to make storage spaces easy to access. In this chapter you'll find suggested
dimensions for making built-in seats comfortable and functional
and ideas for how to build in seating even if your home doesn't
have a bay window for a window seat or a bump-out for a
breakfast nook.

**The best of both
worlds could well be
a breakfast table with
a built-in banquette
on two sides and
conventional seats on
the other two sides.**

built-in seating fits in every room

● ● ● A PLACE TO SIT IN AN ENTRYWAY IS CLOSE to being a necessity. Making it a built-in seat gives it architectural weight and can make the entryway more welcoming in both look and function. People don't sit on an entryway bench for a long time, unlike a breakfast bench, so it doesn't need the overhanging lip that's recommended on an eating seat. A built-in bench in the bathroom adds spa-like comfort and can be a safety feature, offering a slip-free place to dry off. A bathroom seat needn't be cushioned if it's in a damp or wet location, of course. Bedrooms, living spaces, and even workplaces are ideal rooms for built-in seats. Building a seat by a window is a natural, but no one would object if you tucked a built-in seat into a cozy niche on an inside wall.

Built-in seating offers an opportunity for extra storage, but take care to be practical. A hinged top over a bin is a common feature, but what will you store there? This could be a great place for items that are big or seasonal, such as extra throws or pillows, or even a frequently used item, such as a vacuum cleaner, but only if you can easily remove the cushion and open the top. Just don't allow a storage bin to be a catchall for things of any size. Built-in seat bins in houses with small children should be lockable so kids aren't tempted to hide for fun. An expensive but much tidier storage option is to fit a built-in seat with drawers that can be accessed from the front, in the case of a window seat or entryway bench, or from the ends, in the case of kitchen booths. An alternative is to simply design built-in seating as a bench, which can then be kept clear or fit with like-size baskets or decorative boxes, with handles to make them easy to access.

A walnut built-in offers all kinds of mudroom storage, from cubbies to hooks and two levels of shoe storage below the padded bench. Upper shoe shelves are adjustable, and the lower ledge makes it a little easier for all ages to tie shoes.

ABOVE A built-in seat doesn't require a window, especially a seat with a Moorish theme. This reading niche, in a teenage girl's room, is painted a richer shade of lime than the primary walls to make it seem deeper. Its curvy profile is repeated in the headboard.

RIGHT Two closets create a space for a sunny built-in window seat. There's room for shallow storage under the cushion, and the tall toespace allows heat to flow from the radiator under the window.

ABOVE A built-in seat for one is a practical addition to any bathroom. Here, built-in cabinetry creates a sheltered niche. Painted paneling makes a sturdier surface than drywall. Rather than drill continuous holes for adjustable shelves, the cabinetmaker drilled three holes on each side, a more discreet but still flexible option.

built-in seating for breakfast nooks

● ● ● WE USUALLY THINK "BREAKFAST NOOK" when we think of built-ins for dining, but built-in seats for eating can work for any and all meals. A spacious dining room is great for dinner parties and holidays, but the so-called breakfast nook is often a family's favorite place to eat. That's because built-in seating can be cozier and more comfortable than the dining room. Built-in seating is most commonly designed with two benches facing each other, but other options are U-shaped, L-shaped, or one-sided, with conventional chairs pulled up to the opposite side. U-shaped banquettes are wonderfully cozy and allow you to squeeze in one more person, but can also be hard to access (and somehow the first one in always needs to get out first).

One-sided built-in seating allows more flexibility in table size and position and makes it easier to pull a high chair up to the table. Unless you like easing into your seat the way you sit at a picnic table, choose a pedestal table, which won't interfere with your legs. A two-sided nook allows for the table to be attached to the wall at one end for extra stability, but a freestanding table can be moved out for easier cleaning. Provide outlets nearby to plug in laptops for the times when the breakfast nook becomes the homework or work station, and consider where those cords will have to go comfortably and safely.

This breakfast booth seems like a cozy place to eat, but it's more than that. The architects/owners turned this bench into a storage unit from top to bottom. Booth backs glide on full-extension drawer slides assisted by cabled counterweights at the ends. The last bit of space at each booth top is taken over by a long skinny drawer. The table is supported by a heavy metal base with skateboard wheels at the back and stops on the front; just lift the front edge of the table to roll the table out for cleaning.

SIZING UP A BREAKFAST NOOK

The traditional breakfast booth

A breakfast nook with benches requires a pedestal or trestle table, or in a two-sided booth like this, the table can be supported by the wall on one end and a central leg near the other end.

For bench length, figure on about 24 in. per adult for comfort.

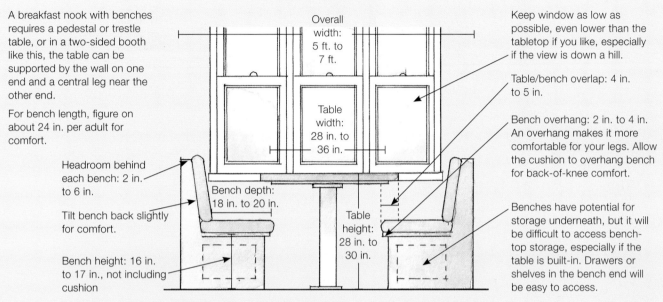

Overall width: 5 ft. to 7 ft.

Table width: 28 in. to 36 in.

Headroom behind each bench: 2 in. to 6 in.

Bench depth: 18 in. to 20 in.

Tilt bench back slightly for comfort.

Table height: 28 in. to 30 in.

Bench height: 16 in. to 17 in., not including cushion

Keep window as low as possible, even lower than the tabletop if you like, especially if the view is down a hill.

Table/bench overlap: 4 in. to 5 in.

Bench overhang: 2 in. to 4 in. An overhang makes it more comfortable for your legs. Allow the cushion to overhang bench for back-of-knee comfort.

Benches have potential for storage underneath, but it will be difficult to access bench-top storage, especially if the table is built-in. Drawers or shelves in the bench end will be easy to access.

Other ways to configure built-in breakfast nooks

Allow at least 32 in. to 36 in. between any wall/cabinet and end of bench/edge of table.

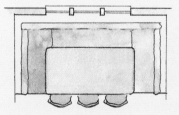

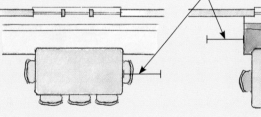

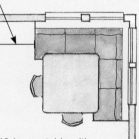

36-in. by 72-in. table with a bench on three sides

More bench seating allows for more sitters, especially if they are kid-sized.

36-in. by 72-in. table with a single straight bench

This configuration is more flexible but may not fit quite as many people as the three-sided bench.

48-in.-sq. table with a corner bench

This configuration is both cozy and flexible.

A built-in breakfast nook is good for much more than breakfast. It often becomes the most popular spot in the house. It's important to locate electrical outlets in a convenient spot for plugging in laptops. This breakfast nook has outlets in two locations.

FACING PAGE
Which side to choose:
the cushy padded
banquette or the
seats with a view?
Either choice works
at this beautiful
informal dining area.

This oceanfront home
is new, with an open
plan that includes a
cozy corner seating
area that opens to
both family room and
kitchen. But details
such as beadboard
on the booth back,
frame-and-panel on
the seat face below,
and the proportions
of the windows
replicate those in
traditional Cape
Cod homes.

• a bench as comfortable as a favorite dining chair

A built-in bench for seating should feel like a comfortable chair, positioned at a comfortable height from the floor and a comfortable angle for the back, at least for adults (see the top drawing on p. 43). Feet should touch the floor, and you should be able to lean back, but not too far. The seat edge shouldn't cut into the back of your knees. Seats should overhang the bench front—if there is one—a few inches so that your legs have room to move;

alternatively, the seat can be shorter from front to back. Allow a few inches beyond the seat back for your head. If you can add a few more inches to make room for shelves—one side or two—you will create a display space for favorite objects or a library for cookbooks. That's only if your breakfast nook is not in a bump-out. If you've got the option for three walls of windows, take it. That way, everyone has a view.

window seats

● ● ● COMPARED TO BUILT-IN SEATING FOR dining, window seats aren't easy to prescribe in terms of size, shape, and detailing. That's because window seats may have different functions. A window seat can provide extra seating for a large gathering in the living room, or it can be a place of solitude where one person can curl up to read, knit, or just enjoy the view. A window seat can double as a guest bed or a favorite spot to nap. If the seat is 18 in. high, including the cushion, it will be comfortable not only for solo reading or napping but as conventional seating when you need it. How wide you make your window seat depends on the space available and how many people will use it. Consider dropping the ceiling to the top of the window trim to make the window seat a cozier spot and to bounce light from the window into the room.

Looking out the window requires sitting at least sideways, so provide a back—at least 15 in. tall—for leaning. The exception would be a window seat with windows on three sides. Loose pillows or custom-fit cushions can make it comfortable to lean, or slope the wall for extra comfort. Building codes usually require windows at a window seat to be tempered, and for a good reason. The logic is that someone might lean on the window or even stand up on the window seat.

A house in the woods feels as if it's part of the outdoors, especially from this window seat in the south-facing living room. The lowered ceiling makes the space cozier, and tall pillows make sitting up to read comfortable. Leaving the seat open underneath allows storage in baskets that are easy to slide out.

BELOW Wood-paneled walls and a lowered ceiling set off a built-in seat to create a nest-like space. The seat is designed for reading or napping, but it's also big enough for a guest bed. The wall literally takes color and material from the natural surroundings. The recessed display niche takes advantage of the thick wall.

ABOVE It makes sense that this west-facing living room on San Juan Island would have its largest windows on the sunset side, and a bump-out with a built-in seat is a natural there, too. The Douglas fir seat contains plenty of drawer storage.

RIGHT Although it's primarily a seat for people, this wall-to-wall built-in seat is a sunny home to potted plants by the window.

A window seat in a bump-out niche has recessed lighting for night-time reading. The window wall is divided into fixed upper windows and double-hung lower windows in the proportion of traditional Eastern seacoast houses. Seat height is set at 16 in. to allow room for a comfy seat cushion, but there's still enough room below for inset drawers.

window seat doesn't need a bump-out

In this bedroom, closets at right and left of a pair of big double-hung windows created an opportunity to build in a window seat, which also acts as a step up to the door at left. Storage in the window-seat compartment is under the two-part hinged seat. A built-in dresser at far left provides even more storage space.

A BUILT-IN WINDOW SEAT WITHOUT A BUMP-OUT

If bumping out an exterior wall isn't possible or desirable, consider tucking a window-seat niche between interior walls. A clothes/coat closet or a workspace niche is deep enough to accommodate a window seat niche.

Lower the ceiling over the niche to match the door height for added coziness, or leave the window-seat ceiling high for drama.

If built-in shelves face the niche, allow 15 in. to 18 in. of solid wall for back support.

Consider framing a window-seat niche with trim for durability and to match door trim.

Build the window seat to about 15 in. to 16 in. above finished floor (assuming a 3-in. to 4-in. cushion on top) or to the height that suits you. If the seat will double as a bed, design it to fit a standard mattress and adjust the height and width accordingly. And consider the location of window trim and hardware if you are using a mattress.

entryways, hallways, and stairways

4

● ● ●

THE CENTER-HALL COLONIAL AND THE FARMHOUSE MUDROOM lean-to are utilitarian ancestors of contemporary entryways, but what distinguishes today's adaptations is an emphasis on built-ins to handle the tasks of coming and going. Sure, the entryway can be simply an unarticulated air chamber between the intemperate outside and the comfortable inside, but today it's more likely to be the home of a bench-cum-footlocker, a multitude of cubbies (or even lockers), along with shelves, pegs, hooks, and other built-in elements. And these built-ins can be off-the-shelf or custom-designed to ease the tasks of getting ready for school, work, and inclement weather and to make it a blessing to come home after a long day in the snow or at a desk. Rather than just looking like the hall closet turned inside out, the entryway—whether at the front door or the back—is a style maven, with details and finishes that rival even the formal living room and the former built-in queen, the kitchen.

It's not just the entryway that benefits from a bounty of built-ins. Other passages in a home can be improved with cabinets, shelves, and seating. A mere hallway can be elevated to a capital-H Hall by making it a foot or two wider to create a valuable space not only for storage but for lingering and for display. Of course, a stairway is a natural for both storage and drama. Treads can be extended beyond the railing for displaying art objects or, at the entryway, to act as landing spaces for library books and backpacks. The underbelly of the stair can be carved out for drawers, shelves, or even a tiny workspace that can be closed off with a door.

This sweet entryway to the back of a cottage is now the primary entrance. It's finished with white-painted MDF beadboard and trim and built-ins for outerwear and entryway essentials. The door at right goes to a small coat closet.

any entryway will do

● ● ● THERE'S THE FRONT DOOR, THEN THERE'S the door everyone uses, close to the car, and that ideally opens onto a space for kicking off snowy boots and hanging up coats and backpacks. In more and more homes, the front entry area *is* the mudroom, or the front entry connects by hallway to a mudroom, a smart way to let built-ins do double duty. A strictly formal front-door entrance itself can gain utility, comfort, and beauty with built-ins: seating, shelving, and perhaps a hallstand for umbrellas and guests' coats or a traditional coat closet for keeping coats and gear out of sight. To keep a single-entrance home tidy, consider adding those built-in elements that make up a mudroom but finish them off with doors and drawers. Even the narrowest of built-ins—a 4-in. shelf at elbow height for keys and sunglasses, 8-in. shelves for books just above head height, a 4-ft.-long Shaker peg board for coats—can add yards of convenience to a narrow apartment entryway.

Here's an entryway to spend some time in. The built-in seat with a toespace opening for heat helps with putting on and taking off boots, but makes a cozy reading niche, too. Built-in cabinets hold baskets for small items, and hooks are handy for seasonal wear. A plate rail above the hooks offers display space.

LEFT Handsome cabinetry gives front-door storage a formal elegance. Multiple layers and storage types offer closed and open storage, including plenty of seating with shoe storage below, cubbies for hats, gloves, and mail.

ABOVE Handling entryway storage in a tight space requires ingenuity. This urban entry closet is 6 ft. wide and outfitted with clothes rods and shelves along one wall (behind the drawers) and hooks on the back wall, just visible in the photo. The sliding door runs to the ceiling, so when closed it looks like a wall, allowing the display shelving and recessed drawers to the right to become the focal point.

LEFT Built-ins at the front door don't need to be tucked away, as this urban townhouse entrance hallway shows. Storage is almost all open, except for seasonal flipper-door cabinets at the top.

CHECKLIST FOR ENTRYWAY BUILT-INS

determine just what built-in details work best for you, but keep in mind that easy-to-use components keep things neater. It's not just the grade-school crowd that prefers hanging casual coats, scarves, and hats on hooks or pegs rather than on hangers. And open cubbies, baskets, and shelves make for speedier storage and retrieval than drawers. Here are some suggestions for entryway built-ins:

- Choose hooks, slots, or a dedicated basket on an elbow-height surface for things that are easily misplaced, like keys and sunglasses.

- Provide a tabletop or an easy-to-access cubby for temporary items, such as outgoing mail and library books.
- Build in a place to charge electronics for everyone in the family; this can be a central strip of outlets or outlets in individual cubbyholes or lockers.
- Hooks for hanging the current season's coats, jackets, scarves, and hats.
- Hooks for backpacks.
- A place for this season's sports gear.
- A place for wet boots.

- A place to sit for putting on and taking off shoes or to wait for the last one downstairs.
- Consider wainscoting or even full-height paneling as part of full-height built-ins or behind lower built-ins because it is easy to clean and hard to damage.
- Space for storing or using pet accessories, such as leashes, kennels, and food and water bowls.

A modest-size mudroom provides a movable bench, built-in rows of hooks, a stack of shelves for glove/hat baskets and shoes, and a two-tiered open closet space for jackets. Two hooks by the door to the kitchen allow for quick storage of everyday items.

LEFT A big family needs big built-ins for their comings and goings. This space has a seat flanked by drawers and landing spaces. Behind the white double doors is a coat closet for the bulk of family outerwear, while hooks on door fronts are for what's needed now. And there's plenty of room for corralling shoes, no longer scattered over the house. Each shelf holds two large trays, which contain any leftover water or debris.

BELOW Anyone who lives in a four-season climate appreciates abundant space for footwear of all kinds and room to sit down and tie laces or pull on boots, especially when guests come often and stay for a while. Easy-to-use hooks for coats are essential.

ABOVE An East Coast cottage received an add-on to make a year-round house more livable for a growing family. Now each household member can claim a storage stall in this generous mudroom, complete with a clothes rod, hooks, and space for shoes and boots.

a place to sit

●●● A PLACE TO SIT IS A NECESSITY IN ANY entryway, but especially in a mudroom, where it may take some effort to put on and remove boots. A built-in bench allows for closed storage beneath, if desired, and adds a sense of comfort and permanence to an entry. If the wall behind the bench is used for hanging coats or backpacks on pegs, make the bench deep enough to sit without having to fight for room. Consider your own family's comfort when sizing up bench dimensions, and see Chapter 3 for details and recommendations.

This simple bench is plenty wide enough for sitting when putting on boots. Cubbies and benchtop have polyurethaned plywood surfaces with contrasting painted solid-wood edgeband. Top cubbies can be reached by standing on the bench.

ABOVE This mudroom has finishes that are tough but easy to clean, and its generous built-in seating with storage drawers give all the family room to move and store their never-ending gear.

RIGHT An entryway fit for spring and summer living is a bright and airy space, thanks to big windows, a screen door, and white-painted woodwork on all surfaces (except the polyurethaned wood floor, of course). The top two shelves in the built-in cabinet are adjustable but the lower two are fixed, with two drawers inset below.

A mudroom that's cheery enough to linger in has a cushioned seat with pillows and no hanging coats to contend with, allowing for a leisurely sit. Cabinets are birch plywood with fixed shelves.

mudrooms

● ● ● MUDROOM BUILT-INS CAN MAKE COMINGS and goings so much easier. A comfortable mudroom should be at least 5 ft. wide, with room for one person to sit on a bench to put on shoes and another person to pass by. That 2-ft. bench space becomes the envelope for a wall of built-ins, with individual cubbies, lockers, or hooks for backpacks and coats (or both personal cubbies and ganged hooks) and with room for sports equipment and other items, such as umbrellas and dog leashes. Space under the bench and against the wall can be handy for shoes, but consider building a version of the Japanese *getabako*, with cubbyholes dedicated to shoe storage. Although closed storage may look tidy, storage for outerwear requires ventilation in just about any climate, so provide ventilation in closed cubbies and shoe or glove/scarf footlockers. But it's easier just to keep built-in mudroom storage open to view and air. A window makes a doubly appreciated addition to a mudroom, adding light and ventilation.

Because the mudroom is close to the car, make sufficient landing space for temporary storage of items such as packages, groceries, and outgoing library books. Of course, make a built-in space on a hook or in a basket for the family keys, the household item that foils too many getaways. A larger mudroom can offer dedicated space under a bench or on deep shelves for recycling bins, allowing space for a paper shredder next to the mixed paper bin, so that constant credit-card mail doesn't have far to travel. A communal charging station, or outlets in individual cubbies, is almost essential in today's mudroom.

mudroom washup

Although a washer and dryer would be a blessing in or near the mudroom, they aren't a necessity, but a sink is a mighty handy built-in to have. For dog owners, a low shower is ideal.

LEFT There's no better place to hose down a dirty dog than in the mudroom. This built-in tiled shower has controls set low but features a long hose and a tall curb.

RIGHT This mudroom is as elegant as a kitchen and makes use of the same good-looking—and tough—materials. The bench is made from quartz that's much tougher than wood and is easy to clean. The stainless-steel sink has an integral backsplash on three sides to offer extra splash protection.

RIGHT A mudroom off the garage isn't just for storage. Inside the tall cabinet to the left of the sink are a stacked washer and dryer, and the good-size sink has a countertop that handles gardening tasks or laundry.

SPORTS EQUIPMENT

here isn't a sport that doesn't lend itself to mudroom built-in storage, so make room for the sport du jour and for other seasons' sports if possible. Install hooks of appropriate size and strength for mitts, racquets, helmets, hats, outerwear, golf bags, and skates, and add specialized hooks for skis, snowboards, and skateboards.

Custom built-in bins for bulky items are handy, but inexpensive off-the-shelf wire holders for balls, bats, lacrosse sticks, and the like can be easily affixed to properly blocked mudroom walls. Paneling is a big plus here for its durability and ease of cleaning and repair.

BELOW A dedicated closet for sports gear is worth its space if it enhances household harmony. This shallow closet is divvied up into shelves, racks, and cages to handle several seasons' worth of balls, racquets, and mitts.

ABOVE Floor-to-ceiling cabinets in this mudroom include tall cubbies outfitted to store skis safely and securely, during ski season and offseason, too. Ski boots have a home at the bottom of the cubbies.

ABOVE AND RIGHT Two built-in cabinets with closed storage—doors, shelves, drawers—anchor the room, one at the back and one near the entrance to the mudroom at right. Two tall cubbies sit on a bench that spans most of the exterior wall, and these are fitted with shelves and pegs. The beadboard-paneled recess opposite the bench contains a row of pegs and a column of shelves with outlets.

LEFT A built-in bench runs from wall to wall in this mudroom, with the section near the door open below for tucking boots and shoes underneath. The frame-and-panel drawers corral loose hats and small outerwear items.

stairways and hallways

●●● A STAIRCASE IS THE ULTIMATE BUILT-IN, but it can also be a container or canvas for built-in storage or display, as long as safety is not compromised. The stair structure takes up space, of course, but unless the drama of a staircase depends on it being open underneath, you've got room to plan for shelves, drawers, or even a small workspace. You may see supposedly clever storage ideas for storing items—shoes or books, for example—under treads and accessible from the open riser or for building drawers in the riser space, but don't be tempted. It's too easy for someone to leave a drawer slightly open or for an errant book to protrude, only to create a serious tripping hazard. Instead, consider storage built into the side of the stair or under the landing. In every case, check building codes to see if materials can be stored under a staircase.

Although risers don't make good storage, the midway point of a switchback staircase is a magical place to be, and it's especially so if a built-in seat with a window takes up residence. A cushion is a given here, and shelves carved into the stud space make for a small personal library.

Any bit of unused wall space will do for built-in storage. These simple inset drawers won't interfere with traffic.

LEFT AND ABOVE The staircase in a renovated townhouse in Boston received a complete makeover inside and out. The lower display and bookshelf is a front for a big bin that slides out (you can see one of the two handles) for access to household goods, from paper towels to lightbulbs. The topmost shelf slides out, too, with hidden storage for small items.

make a hallway a destination

A hall doesn't have to be wasted space. Instead, add narrow display or bookshelf built-ins to an existing hall, or carve shelf space from between studs for displaying small objects. Or add 18 in. to 2 ft. to a hall in your not-yet-built dream house. With good lighting, a built-in bench, cabinets or shelves, and even a desk, that hall can become a room of its own, operating as a home office, homework station, or simply a cozy reading nook. To make both an adjacent public room and a hallway seem more spacious, open the wall between them from about countertop height to door-frame height and finish the opening with a wide shelf as a pass-through.

A multitasking hallway links kids' bedrooms with their bathroom (look for the green pocket door to the bathroom) and with the kitchen, a laundry space, and an outdoor terrace. The room-size hall has workspace for two; when work is done, desks fold down to look like paneling.

ABOVE In a major makeover of a plain ranch house into a bungalow, the fireplace is one of the few remaining parts. A new hallway, with its Arts and Crafts flavor, transforms the entry and living room with hefty beams, square columns, and frame-and-panel cabinets, as well as a warmly lit built-in seat that invites a longer stay than most entry-hall benches.

LEFT This upstairs window seat is deep (2 ft. 6 in.) and has a solid back wall for reading. Recessed shelves are designed as a visual extension of the windows, with the same trim and finish.

A single stair tread stretches out and turns the corner to become an entryway bench and a window seat. In keeping with the diminutive size of the cottage, a modest built-in shelf with hooks makes handy storage for today's jackets.

ABOVE Every bit of usable space under this stair has been put to good use for entryway storage.

ABOVE A Texas stair takes inspiration from traditional Japanese *kaidan dansu,* or step chests, wood boxes that stack together in a pleasing composition to make both stair and storage.

LEFT A switchback stair creates a perfect location for a built-in seat and bookshelves. The bench seat bows out a bit to add depth and a gentle flourish.

kitchens and dining

● ● ●

OF ALL THE ROOMS IN YOUR HOUSE, THE KITCHEN IS THE PRIME SPACE for built-ins. Kitchen activities require lots of storage, so lots of cabinets and shelves are a given. Cabinets provide organized and often specialized places to store tools, dishes, cookware, and food. You need countertops for working, so you're likely to have mostly base cabinets and, often, shallower wall cabinets. Sometimes upper cabinets aren't attached to walls at all, but span between walls (over an island, for example) or are attached to the ceiling.

Don't overlook that practical built-in, the open shelf, and note that shelves also add character and texture to a kitchen. Shelves can amplify the feeling of spaciousness or do exactly the opposite and add a sense of comfort and intimacy, especially to a dining area. Shelves can be designed to practically disappear or offer a hefty presence, depending on style and function. And shelves are what make a pantry, whether in-cabinet or built into a closet.

Dining spaces themselves can be built-in, but built-ins can embellish dining spaces in other ways. Consider a dining-specific built-in such as a hutch, corner cabinet, or sideboard, but don't overlook the utility, beauty, and embracing coziness of bookshelves or a window seat in the dining room.

A critical question is where to place those big built-ins: appliances. Once you've established where primary appliances and workspaces go, built-ins can fill in to create storage and comfort, crafting a kitchen that's both fun and easy to work in.

A colorful assembly of built-ins makes this kitchen warm and cheerful. Cabinets are green, white, or natural, all with the same pulls and hinges. Small drawers are single-panel, and big drawers have frame-and-panel faces. Storage is closed except for the open display shelf combined with vertical plate slots and flatware drawers.

shaping the kitchen with built-ins

● ● ● RATHER THAN STUFFING A KITCHEN WITH as many built-ins as possible, give that bulk some breathing room, not only for looks but for function. For example, corner cabinets are notorious for being hard to outfit for easy access, so why not run cabinets to the wall instead of around the inside corner? You'll "lose" very little storage volume and will gain easier access. Yes, you'll lose some countertop space, but make that up with a fold-down surface or a rolling cart. Consider leaving off upper cabinets over an island between the kitchen and dining/family space to increase the perceived volume of the room. If you prefer to delineate the edge of the kitchen, or you simply need more storage or display space, use glass doors on those upper cabinets to share light but still define the kitchen space. Doors on each side of these cabinets allow double access, too.

Think of wall cabinets as optional. Give precedence to views of the outdoors and to connecting kitchen to dining or family spaces, and reserve wall cabinets for other walls. Open shelves, even across a window, can be lighter, brighter, and make the kitchen seem bigger, all while offering more space to store things.

No wall cabinets interfere with the beautiful window wall, but there are plenty of cabinets floor to ceiling on the side walls. Cabinets in the refrigerator wall take on a more heavy-duty utilitarian character, with polished nickel latches on upper cabinets and the pantry, far left. To allow for seating, the marble countertop overhangs the cabinet and is supported by brackets on each end.

ABOVE A comfy place to sit near the back door in a kitchen is just right for shedding boots in the winter and ideal for anyone who wants to be in the kitchen but out of the way of cooking.

BELOW A renovated dining/kitchen area opens up to increase circulation and expand views. This opening connects dining with entryway while also providing storage and a display shelf (see pp. 18 and 75 for kitchen views).

An urban West Coast butler's pantry receives a modern makeover with inset doors and drawers, long wire pulls, and thick shelves. Behind the door at left is a pull-out trash container.

• the triangle lives on

Every so often, the kitchen triangle is scorned as being out of date, but there's still no getting around the fact that it's easier to make dinner if refrigerator, range, and sink are reasonably close to each other. Sure, the range may bifurcate into a cooktop and wall ovens and the big sink into two sinks, or there may be two cooks instead of one, but the principle applies: Keep the tasks of making dinner, serving, and cleanup as easy and straightforward as possible. Imagine yourself (or whomever cooks) making dinner. Go through each step. Where is food stored? Where are tools, such as cutting boards and knives? Are colanders near a sink? Are dishes stored near the serving area? Not everyone's cooking style is the same, but the rule of thumb is to cluster appliances reasonably close together, using built-ins to increase the flow, not interrupt it. Position an island to one side so that it's easy to get between sink and cooktop, or make that island itself a destination—put the cooktop there, or the sink. Steer noncooking traffic away from the heat of cooking. One trick that helps is to locate the refrigerator on the outskirts of the kitchen, close to the eating space.

Pantry, refrigerator, range, and sink (at right, but not in view) are close enough together for comfortable cooking in this renovated family kitchen. Cabinetry surrounding the freestanding refrigerator is extra deep to make the standard-depth model look built in.

ABOVE This modest-size U-shaped kitchen benefits from avoiding a built-in island and going for a rolling butcher-block cart instead. The cart can move anywhere, either as extra space or for prep, serving, or collecting dirty dishes from the nearby dining table.

BUILDING IN SPACE FOR GARBAGE AND RECYCLING

municipalities often have different requirements for recycling, so design or renovate your kitchen to fit your particulars and to suit your work habits. Would you prefer to dump recyclables from a smaller bin in the kitchen into the bin that goes outside on recycling/garbage day? Or would you prefer to store the outside recycling bins themselves in or near the kitchen? Although it's common, garbage and/or recycling located under the sink can become a real source of conflict during cleanup, even if one person is doing the cleanup. Consider locating garbage or recycling bins on one side of the big sink and the dishwasher on the other side. Or locate garbage just across the aisle, but not in a major path. And you'll want the garbage bin and/or compost pail near to where you prepare dinner. Make it easy to open, say, with your foot or with a touch latch operated by your knee or the back of your hand.

RIGHT AND ABOVE It may be spacious, but this kitchen is efficient, with its three major points—sink, fridge, and cooktop—close together and supported by plenty of adjacent countertop space. The center three of six 58-ft. bow trusses salvaged from the Nashville recording studio where Elvis recorded "Heartbreak Hotel" determined the location of the kitchen, mostly made up of base cabinets in two long islands.

ABOVE AND RIGHT This renovated farm-house kitchen has room for five to sit at one end of the generous island, but the working end is packed with drawers and offers uninterrupted counter space. The tall cabinets against the back wall aren't workspaces, so are trimmed with baseboard.

m o r e   a b o u t . . .
UNIVERSAL DESIGN

he term, "universal design" covers design that makes life easier for people of all abilities, not just the average person. Although it's especially important with baby boomers reaching retirement age, design for access isn't just for older people. Universal design recommendations for the kitchen include these pretty easy suggestions: Keep the microwave oven controls no higher than 48 in. above the floor; keep most storage between 15 in. and 48 in. from the floor; offer two work-

counter heights—one 28 in. to 36 in. high and one 36 in. to 45 in. above the floor—and choose a single-lever or hands-free faucet. Raise the dishwasher, washer, and dryer 6 in. to 12 in. above the floor to improve access for people who may not be as mobile. But wouldn't that make life easier for everyone? For more recommendations, including how to accommodate a wheelchair in the kitchen, see "Comfortable Dining Dimensions," p. 81, and Resources, p. 166.

•sizing up
kitchen built-ins

Although a super-slim galley kitchen may have a 38-in. aisle, that's not room enough for two to work comfortably. An aisle that's between 42 in. and 48 in. allows appliance doors to open and creates breathing room for two cooks or a cook and assistant. If the aisle is much wider, it's harder to work efficiently. Position an island so that it improves flow rather than makes for more steps.

Removing a wall between dining and kitchen gave this once cramped galley kitchen just a bit more room but a lot more perceived space, as well as access from both sides of the cabinets.

fitting in appliances

●●● NEW APPLIANCE MODELS ARE OFFERED on a regular basis, so this book can't cover the latest in fuel source or finish guidelines, but instead offers tips on how to fit appliances into cabinetry (see "Locating Built-In Appliances" on pp. 78–79). Whatever the appliance, think ahead about where it fits in the cabinetry (or not) in terms of appearance and sequence of work. For example, will the appliance be hidden? Will it be flush with the cabinetry? Should it be raised for easier operation? If you are starting from scratch, don't put off choosing appliances until the last minute. Cabinet sizes and configuration and electrical and plumbing layouts depend on the specifications of the appliances you select. If you are replacing appliances but not cabinets, look for appliances that will fit with little or no jury rigging.

Consider how appliance doors will interact with cabinet doors or drawers. A fridge too close to a wall won't open all the way. A dishwasher too close to a corner might prohibit a drawer from opening. Appliances need landing spaces, too. In general, each appliance requires a landing space of about 15 in. on one side. Landing spaces for a cooktop will be on both sides, whereas the landing space for a fridge or oven can either be adjacent to it or across an aisle— but no more than 4 ft. away and not across a major route, such as the family's path to the back door. These are minimums, remember. If you like to cook, especially for a family or a crowd, you will want wider landing spaces. And you'll need to combine the minimums if the space is between two appliances.

RIGHT This floor-to-ceiling cabinet creates a butler's pantry in the corner of a dining room. Slim appliances include a below-counter fridge and a wine cooler, and a bar sink adds utility without taking up much real estate.

FACING PAGE Symmetrical cabinets in two heights add formality and focus to the cooktop and handsome hood vent in this kitchen. The sink, set in a standard-height countertop behind the raised bar countertop in the foreground, is directly in line with the cooktop.

LOCATING BUILT-IN APPLIANCES

RANGES

The standard range is 30 in. wide and has four burners and a single oven. Freestanding ranges are the most common type by a long shot, and slide-ins follow in popularity. Some new ranges have two ovens stacked, with one quite thin. A smaller oven cavity improves energy efficiency and moisture retention. Ovens with smaller cavities can be more energy-efficient, allowing you to cook a pizza, a pie, or a single pan of cookies in a smaller space. Wide ovens may have two ovens side by side. Many professional-style ranges are taller and deeper than the typical base cabinet with countertop. Consider setting standard cabinet cases on a higher toekick base to raise the countertop height.

COOKTOPS

An apron-front gas cooktop with heavy grating has a more substantial visual presence in the kitchen, whereas a drop-in smooth-top cooktop practically disappears. The space below the cooktop is often home to a stack of wide drawers for pots and pans, although open shelves work well here, too. Whether cooktops are gas or electric, a cooktop that's placed against a wall allows ventilation to work much more efficiently because the backsplash helps capture steam, smoke, and odors. Cooktops in islands require stronger vent fans and can be a potential hazard for onlookers. Any combustible materials must be at least 30 in. above the surface of a cooktop.

RANGE/COOKTOP VENT HOODS

Give your cooktop the ventilation it needs with a vent hood that's the right size and in the right place. An over-the-range-microwave oven with a vent isn't ideal for people who really like to cook up a storm. If it's still your choice, try to duct it to the outdoors. A ductless hood vent just recirculates heat, smoke, and odors back into your house. Downdraft vents may be sufficient for electric cooktops and moderate cooking. But avid cooks, especially those with gas cooktops, will want vent hoods that do the job. A hood should be 3 in. wider than the cooktop on each side and cover at least 50 percent of the cooktop area. A too-low vent hood is a common complaint. Avoid this by raising the hood and adding a stronger fan. See Resources, p. 166, for a guide to vent-hood sizing. Make sure ducts are smooth and have as few bends as possible. A remote fan will take a big bite out of fan noise.

MICROWAVE OVENS

Microwave ovens may be freestanding or built-in. Built-in microwave ovens are ideally installed just under the countertop in a base cabinet or at countertop height. Consider locating the microwave oven at the perimeter of your work area, available to the cook but also easy to access by the rest of the family. A microwave oven over the range is common, but not ideal, as the microwave will be in the way of cooktop action. A microwave oven over the cooktop should be 18 in. (this is likely a forehead-banging height) to 24 in. (better) over the cooktop, making microwave access comfortable and safe for taller people.

WARMING OVENS/DRAWERS

Some electric ovens have warming drawers built in, but separate warming ovens (or oven drawers) are a welcome addition to an active family with avid cooks and for people who order out frequently. A warming oven keeps foods at a safe, even temperature, but many models offer options to keep food moist or dry (don't count on warming ovens keeping food really crisp). Warming ovens can heat plates and soup bowls, defrost food, and dry breadcrumbs. Just below the countertop and near your serving area is the best location.

REFRIGERATOR

A freestanding fridge is typically 27 in. deep, whereas cabinets are 24 in. deep, so the refrigerator will project 3 in. past the cabinets. If that's not a look you want, consider a built-in refrigerator (the considerably more expensive alternative) or a freestanding cabinet-depth fridge. The shallow depth of these 24-in. fridges makes it easier to locate items, but also may prevent the use of large platters. All the more reason to measure your dishes and take those measurements to the appliance showroom, as it's tough to really tell refrigerator configurations online or in a catalog. Another way around this is to set standard cabinets 3 in. away from the wall to align with a standard fridge. The countertop will be deeper, of course, and you'll need to review what else goes in that particular stretch of cabinetry.

WINE COOLERS/CHILLERS

A built-in wine cooler (also called a wine chiller or a wine refrigerator) is usually 24 in., the size of a dishwasher, and holds 28 to 60 bottles, depending on bottle size. Built-in models can be stainless steel, and some offer the potential to trim the door or shelves to match cabinets. Although a built-in wine cooler vents out the front, note that freestanding models usually vent out the rear and should not be built into cabinetry. You might want to locate a wine cooler near dining, but be aware that a wine cooler makes some noise, like any refrigerator.

DISHWASHERS

A dishwasher is placed to either side of the major sink with dish storage nearby, ideally, making it a one-step process to empty the dishwasher. For a concealed dishwasher, care must be taken to make sure the dishwasher is installed at the right depth, so that the applied panel matches the adjacent cabinetry. Dishwasher drawers can be stacked or placed on each side of the sink. Separating the drawers means there's no need to bend over to unload the dishwasher, but it costs more due to additional plumbing and electrical work.

SINKS

A big kitchen sink that allows a cookie sheet to sit flat is likely a better choice for cooks than a multi-bowl sink with rounded edges, which can restrict what goes in the sink. Of course, a second sink for food prep or at a bar is a blessing. Make that second sink at least big enough to handle a colander or to comfortably wash fragile stemware. Sinks can be mounted under the counter (undermount), integral with the countertop (e.g., stainless steel or solid surface; no seams to clean!), or dropped into the countertop. A farmhouse, or apron-front, sink sticks out a bit from the base cabinet and its fittings are commonly installed in the strip of countertop between sink and backsplash. These models allow you to belly right up to the sink and reach deeper into the bowl. Fittings for sinks can be mounted into the sink itself, or in the case of some drop-ins and all undermount sinks, into the countertop. Consider installing a motion-sensor faucet or a foot-pedal-operated faucet, which allows you to wash hands without touching anything.

This narrow space between the dining area and an existing wall is just big enough for a dishwasher and sink. The 36-in.-high countertop could have been extended all the way to the dining area, but creating a raised shelf near the dining table hides dirty dishes, and no counter space is lost. The farmhouse apron-front sink is a small model, and its single bowl makes sense in a small kitchen, as it can fit a stack of dirty pots and pans.

dining space built-ins

● ● ● AS THE HEART OF THE HOUSE, THE KITCHEN is naturally where built-in seating is a high priority. Built-in breakfast-nook (banquette) seating is discussed in depth in Chapter 3. In this chapter you'll find suggestions for where to place any kind of built-in seating, and additional information for breakfast-bar/island seating, and even for nonseating built-ins that can improve dining spaces. The National Kitchen and Bath Association® (NKBA) recommends that for a seating area where no through traffic passes behind a seated diner, allow 32 in. between table or countertop edge and the nearest vertical surface. If traffic will pass behind the seated diner, increase that dimension to 44 in. for a comfortable walk-through. For comfortable dining dimensions, see the sidebar on the facing page.

ABOVE A low bookcase separates the dining room from circulation without closing off the sightlines, and its generous wood surface offers space on top for items going out, for display, or for buffet dishes, depending on the need.

BELOW This dining room built-in shows off stacks of crafting material, evidence of another use for the dining room table. The beefy, complex wall base wraps the cabinet to accentuate its permanence.

ABOVE A faceted window seat adds extra seating to the dining room, and its inset drawers provide storage for linens. Building codes require electrical outlets at regular intervals, and a window seat is no exception.

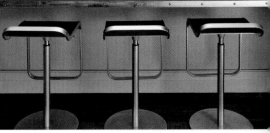

ABOVE A bank of windows in an urban apartment makes an ideal spot for built-in bar seating, a nice change from the usual island bar seating.

COMFORTABLE DINING DIMENSIONS

	COUNTER HEIGHT	KNEE-SPACE DEPTH	WIDTH PER SEAT	SEAT HEIGHT
Table dining	28 in. to 30 in.	18 in.	24 in.	18 in. to 19 in.
Standard countertop height	36 in.	15 in.	24 in.	24 in. to 26 in.
Bar height	42 in.	12 in.	24 in.	30 in.
Universal design access for wheelchair	27 in. to 34 in.	17 in. at feet, 11 in. at knees	36 in.	NA

built-in islands

● ● ● AS A DESCENDENT OF THE FARM OR colonial keeping-room table, the island has never really gone out of style, but the built-in version is a more recent kitchen staple. A built-in kitchen island can simply be a cluster of cabinets topped by a countertop, or it can include appliances, a sink, and bar seating.

Providing dining space on two sides of an island's corner allows diners to see and chat with each other, whereas single-line bar-style seating may suit the early-morning diner who prefers more space to stretch out the paper and have that first cup of coffee. An island can be as thin or as wide as you'd like, but less than 18 in. isn't useful for most kitchen tasks. If the short side of an island is over 5 ft., you'll have a tough time reaching the center, and the island's expanse will impede speedy food preparation.

If a tight budget and small space warrant, you can save money and space by forgoing the built-in aspect. A free-floating island, such as a butcher-block cart, can provide workspace and even storage space but costs much less than a fixed island, which requires at least electrical service, if not other utilities. And it makes a smaller kitchen more flexible.

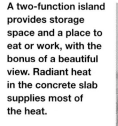

A two-function island provides storage space and a place to eat or work, with the bonus of a beautiful view. Radiant heat in the concrete slab supplies most of the heat.

LEFT This industrial-strength built-in island framed by pipes and sporting plywood-box shelves is balanced by more traditional, highly finished frame-and-panel upper and base cabinets along the walls. The well-populated pot rack is suspended from ceiling joists.

RIGHT The business side of this eating/working island contains a cooktop with ample granite landing space on each side. On the dining side of the island, a stretch of butcher block is anchored in place to serve as the countertop. Simple and elegant frosted-glass flipper doors finish off wall cabinets.

ABOVE Streamlined surfaces are part modern design and part the result of budget constraints, as the architects and owners pitched in together to build this house on a budget. The island countertop is hot rolled steel coated with epoxy, and the island case is faced with white pine boards.

kitchen cabinets

●●● CABINET BASICS ARE DISCUSSED IN Chapter 2. This chapter offers size and detail suggestions for kitchen cabinets in particular. Base cabinets for kitchens are usually built 34½ in. high to receive a 1½-in. countertop. Of course, custom cabinets can be built to just about any size, but a less expensive way of making taller base cabinets is to set standard-base cabinet cases on high-toespace bases.

Plan cabinets to fit what you own now. Take out the measuring tape early; don't wait until cabinets are installed to discover that your large dinner plates don't fit in the standard 12-in.-deep wall cabinet. Wall cabinets are typically installed at 16 in. to 18 in. above the countertop, but can certainly be installed higher to give the taller cook more headroom. Higher shelves might require a stool for the shorter members of the family. No storage space is lost if you fill the space between countertop and wall cabinets with shallow shelves for spices and hooks for frequently used tools. Stock wall cabinets won't touch the ceiling if installed at standard heights. You can display decorative items up there, or install lighting to dramatic effect. A common detail is to drop the ceiling down to the top of wall cabinets to create a soffit that acts as a chase for utilities.

Kitchen-prep gear finds a convenient spot behind doors under a cooktop. Shallow shelves allow spice jars to be easily seen, grabbed, and replaced. Overlay drawers to the right and left contain bigger tools and a battery of pots and pans.

ABOVE In snow country, maple cabinets, tawny walls, terra cotta colored trim, and cherry flooring heat up the visual temperature. The clean lines of full overlay doors and an arched valance over the window add serenity. Instead of a toekick, island cabinets on the seating side have a flush base and sides are untrimmed panels.

more about...
ADDING LIGHT TO CABINETS AND SHELVES

@s you select built-ins for your kitchen, incorporate lighting from the get-go rather than waiting to tack it on later. Include the three types of lighting: task lighting for safe and easy work, ambient lighting for overall comfort and enjoyment, and accent lighting for highlighting favorite kitchenware. Allow room under wall cabinets to mount light fixtures for task lighting, but understand that a shiny countertop reflects every detail, so install lights along the front edge of cabinets if possible (so you don't see the reflection while seated), or choose a honed or matte countertop finish. Consider lighting the interiors of glass-door cabinets; you'll want glass shelves in this case so the light can travel. Fit a deep pantry cabinet with lighting that turns on when the door is opened. Open shelves benefit from ambient and accent lighting. Plugmold outlets along the underside of a wall cabinet or lower on a backsplash make it easy to use small appliances anywhere.

RIGHT An abundance of white makes color in this cheery urban kitchen pop. White IKEA cabinets show off a collection of 20th-century dishes, and glass shelves allow light to bounce around. The white glass-tile backsplash magnifies the light in contrast to the dark solid-surface countertop.

FACING PAGE Flipper doors on wall cabinets prevent accidental head bumps. A thick wood end wall makes a more substantial end for the run of base cabinets than would a simple end panel.

LEFT AND BELOW Cabinet accessories can simplify life in the kitchen. Here, a pull-out rack keeps spices at hand next to the range, and swing-out hardware makes the dark recesses of the corner cabinet much more accessible. Cabinet doors swing out, fold in half, or flip up and slide in, depending on the need and space available.

ABOVE A thoroughly modern kitchen keeps things streamlined but accessible. A sliding door reveals everyday cooking spices and condiments. Backsplash tiles are stainless steel, as is the countertop.

RIGHT A posse of kitchen tools requires substantial drawer construction, and these two big, dovetailed Craftsman-style drawers are built to suit. Slotted drawer inserts keep knife blades hidden but handles handy, and compartments put a stop to tangled tools in the lower drawer.

•enhancing cabinets, inside and out

Drawers have been a big deal in kitchen cabinetry for a while now, not just for the usual flatter items stored in them—like silverware, knives, wraps, and towels—but for stacks of dishes and pots of all sizes (and their lids), kitchen implements that used to be stored as well as exclusively on racks or on shelves. Storing such bulky items in cabinetry is more expensive than hanging them up or storing them on open shelves, but it does keep them clean.

Style-wise, today's cabinets aren't often elaborately embellished with corbels and other fancy molding, but they can still be elegant. Currently the simple thumb pull and built-in channel have seen a comeback, but these can be more expensive than traditional pulls and knobs. Inside, the cabinet is a different story, as a cabinet can be packed with accessories. Accessories of all kinds are available for sorting small tools, plates, knives, silverware, spices, and more. Although it's best not to cram your kitchen from head to toe with built-in cabinets, there's no reason not to make every inch count inside the cabinet. Door ladders on the inside of cabinet doors can hold spices or other small items, and lift-up or pull-out shelves can make a hard-to-reach base cabinet instantly accessible. As a rule, you can save money by purchasing aftermarket accessories, but it's a bit trickier to retrofit cabinets with more complex hardware.

built-in shelves

● ● ● FOR WELL OVER A CENTURY, HOME economists and ergonomics experts have promoted open shelves as the built-in of choice for kitchens, primarily for practicality. But they also brighten up a kitchen and give it texture and depth. The ideal strategy is to choose a shallow depth wherever practical. This allows you to see what you have and gives favorite objects a place to shine. It doesn't mean all shelves must be narrow; you'll want to store plenty of big items, such as a slow cooker, mixing bowls, or a paella pan. Despite the convenience of open storage, some homeowners prefer their kitchen equipment under wraps. Although drawers seem to have taken over kitchen cabinets for many storage tasks, pull-out shelves can be just as handy for keeping your gear out of sight yet easy to access. See Chapter 2 for more information about sizing, spacing, and supporting shelves.

Form follows function in this kitchen's storage choices. Books and display pieces inhabit open shelves at left, a large collection of dishes are kept dust-free but visible behind lightly frosted glass doors, and all other storage is hidden behind closed doors.

A sliver of space in a Boston townhouse offers enough room for bar cabinetry that's both functional and beautiful. The base cabinet curves out to accommodate a tiny sink and closed-door storage and aligns with a closed cabinet above.

ABOVE In a new kitchen, thin marble shelves span traditional double-hung windows to give them a more contemporary appearance. Shelf supports were notched into framing. A pair of dishwasher drawers flanks each side of the sink.

RIGHT As the centerpiece of a passive-solar house in Virginia, this kitchen simplifies space and storage. Practically all storage resides on shelves in stock IKEA cabinets lightly screened by translucent sliding doors, and the island is home to all appliances. Open bookshelves stretch into dining and living spaces.

pantries

● ● ● PANTRIES COME IN ANY NUMBER OF SHAPES and sizes, so choose whatever space and location works for your needs, budget, and space. Cabinet manufacturers will offer cabinets meant for pantry storage, such as a full-height pull-out pantry unit with a stack of shelves or a floor-to-ceiling same-depth cabinet with pull-out shelves. If you have more floor space, consider a reach-in closet-size pantry, even 2 ft. square, lined with lots of narrow shelves, or a walk-in pantry that can even have extra workspace or a table for cooling pies or cookies out of view. If possible, locate the pantry on a cool wall and give it a louvered door for ventilation. Good lighting is essential, and it's especially handy if the light turns on when you open the door. A shallow fluorescent fixture over the door on the inside, facing the shelves, makes a bright, cool, energy-efficient choice.

For a closet-size space that's fitted as a pantry or for a walk-in pantry, waist-high shelves should be 6 in. to 9 in. deep to make it easy to see what's in storage. Lower shelves can be deeper for bulkier, heavier items. Recycling bins can sit on the floor or on a slightly raised shelf. Store items front to back the way the grocery store does, then side to side. Keep a stepstool handy. Store lighter-weight items higher for safety's sake. Keep in mind that the most useful storage space is between hip height and shoulder height. Some organization guidelines suggest storing like items with like items, but this isn't always efficient. Instead, store items according to how frequently you need to access them.

In a renovated 19th-century home, space between kitchen and dining was reclaimed to make pull-out pantry shelves for wine bottles and a variety of beverages.

RIGHT In keeping with this house's 1890's heritage, the two new built-in pantries that flank the breakfast nook imitate the traditional step-back china cabinet. Doors and drawers are inset and legs are expressed.

ABOVE There's no room for doors to swing open fully in this step-in china pantry, so screens slide down to shield dishes and glassware from dust. Dovetailed drawer boxes are crafted from wood and veneer plywood, whereas shelves are painted MDF and case sides are melamine-clad particleboard.

living spaces

● ● ●

EVEN MORE THAN THE KITCHEN, A LIVING SPACE IS HOME TO A ROOM-stretching variety of activities. That means relaxation and excitement in the same room. There's no better match for what a living room needs than built-in cabinetry. At times theater, library, toy chest, and museum, built-in cabinetry adds utility, beauty, and comfort and is worth every square foot it takes up. For starters, consider built-in seating. Much of living space goes to seating, and built-ins can work beautifully in that department, especially by a window with a great view (see Chapter 3 for built-in seating). But where living-space built-ins excel is in shaping space, adding style, displaying treasures, and housing entertainment gear.

Many of us need storage for traditional, nonelectronic entertainment, including reading and playing card games and board games. And a big family room might offer a billiard table with built-in racks. More and more, though, the gear that generates much of today's entertainment is electronic, and that gear must be housed properly, and, if you prefer, hidden when turned off. A built-in media cabinet does not have to take center stage; in fact, it often shares space or gracefully yields center stage to the traditional focus of a living space, the fireplace and its mantel, hearth, and surround. While media cabinetry and a fireplace are popular built-ins, nothing gives a personal stamp to a living space better than built-in display space for family treasures such as books, artwork, photos, and favorite collections.

A sense of tranquility in this family room comes from the wall-to-wall built-in cabinetry and fireplace. To keep the television from having to be set too high, the firebox is kept low, with a slim limestone hearth. An articulated arm mounted on the wall allows the television to be pulled out and tilted as necessary, away from glare or toward viewers.

shaping living spaces with built-ins

●●● LIVING-SPACE BUILT-INS CAN TRANSFORM a room to allow it to serve multiple functions. Primarily, built-ins can contain focal points, namely the TV or the fireplace, or both, and these focal points guide how you arrange your furniture. Cabinetry can be designed so that bookshelves, a television, and, perhaps, a fireplace are separate units. Or a single built-in can contain shelves, television, and fireplace, if you prefer or if room size makes that choice for you. If you've got a fabulous view, keep built-ins against interior walls or low. Rather than concentrate primarily on a TV screen, make a great view the focus. In this case, place television cabinetry 90 degrees from the window instead of on the wall opposite the view; this helps reduce glare, too. Tall built-ins on interior walls can provide a sense of enclosure and coziness, can block a view that isn't so desirable, and can isolate spaces to give some aural and visual privacy. But it's impossible to isolate TV-watching from homework and other quiet activities. Better to offer a constant TV-watcher a separate room away from the living space and to conceal the living-space TV behind doors in built-in cabinetry.

An urban built-in makes the most of a narrow living room, with ample shelves for books, art, photos, and a niche for a stand-mounted TV. Here's a good reason for adjustable shelves, as the niche can change shape if needed. Baskets make ideal containers for magazines.

LEFT A comfortable living-room corner is dedicated to a built-in bookshelf with flat-screen TV in the center, installed at a good viewing angle for close-by armchairs. Surface-mounted library task lights supplement the ambient room lights tucked into the broad ceiling cove.

LEFT Mahogany bookshelves form one wall of this living room in a North Carolina mountain home, and because the view is too good to miss, a good portion of the cabinetry is open to the entryway. The wood mantel is a streamlined version of Craftsman style.

BELOW Conversation and music are the focus of this living room, with generous seating in the center. Built-in cabinets are set back a few feet to play a supporting role to the fireplace and its decorative stone mantel.

styling
living-space
built-ins

● ● ● LIVING-SPACE BUILT-INS ARE A GREAT WAY to reinforce or even embellish house style. If trim details and proportions from the rest of the house apply to built-in cabinetry, new cabinetry will fit seamlessly into an existing house, and a new house can gain instant charm. In a traditional-style home, classically detailed built-in cabinetry can disguise the trappings of modern life—namely, the TV, the computer, and all that audio equipment—behind doors that are easy to open and equally easy to close. There's really no house style that precludes the use of built-ins in living spaces. For example, modern design depends on built-ins for a streamlined aesthetic, and built-ins are a key ingredient in Craftsman-style houses.

Part of the appeal of built-ins in living spaces is the sense of comfort and permanence they can provide, but if you want to lighten the bulk of a built-in, look for open shelves and glass-paneled doors or a less ornate trim. Glass doors keep dust at bay while still highlighting contents, and in-cabinet lighting showcases displays and adds ambience.

A home with a small footprint makes the most of a tall living space with a sculptural fireplace/ television surround built simply from framing and drywall. Recessed fluorescent lighting above the television and in coves creates ambient light that's both beautiful and efficient. When the TV is not in use for video, a slideshow can fill the screen.

ABOVE Maple built-in cabinets provide contrasting texture to the smooth surface of the projecting fireplace and chimney. Closed cabinets offer room for more books, magazines, and electronics.

LEFT The handsome built-in cabinetry reflects not only the traditional design of this new home, but the 21st-century status of the flat-screen television, as a significant built-in component. CDs and DVDs fit on pull-out shelves behind the glass-door cabinet at left.

RIGHT This house has a small footprint—that of the original cottage—so it grew up instead of out. Its television is tucked in a built-in niche upstairs, overlooking the double-height living room space. Clerestory windows and tempered glass railings amplify light.

the television in the room

●●● FOR CENTURIES, LIVING SPACES HAVE centered on the fireplace out of necessity but also for comfort and looks. But for the last 50-plus years, the television has in many homes worked its way to center stage, or at least to equal billing with the fireplace. Flat-screen televisions have taken that focus to a new level because they are so much wider and thinner than tube-based televisions. Where to put the TV might well be the primary design issue in today's living spaces. One way to solve that question is to separate TV watching from living spaces, putting the television instead in a media room or family room and leaving the living space to the fireplace and conversation. But space may rule out a separate TV room, and many families count on a television screen for living-space activities.

Installing a flat-screen television directly on the wall is one design option, but built-ins are still an agreeable way to house a television as part of an overall composition of display and storage, and make it much easier to conceal wiring.

A television can fit in any built-in, whether it is floor-to-ceiling, wall-to-wall, armoire height, or a low console height that brings to mind the 1960s HiFi console (without the gold-threaded speaker fabric that was fun to pick out when parents weren't looking). A flat-screen TV can be stand-mounted or wall-mounted. A stand mount is simpler and can just rest on a shelf or counter. A wall-mount can be installed on a blank wall or in a built-in niche. You'll want to coordinate room size and arrangement with the design of a built-in cabinet and with the type of television, either plasma or LCD. Both technologies are making strides to overcome any drawbacks, so your choice may come down to size, brand, and cost.

If you're building from scratch, be sure blocking is added between studs where any flat-screen television may be installed; ¾-in. plywood is often attached between studs in the general area where a TV cabinet or television will be installed. In an existing wall, drywall can be cut out and replaced with plywood. Opening up the wall also makes it easier to run cables in the wall.

WHERE TO PLACE A FLAT-SCREEN TV

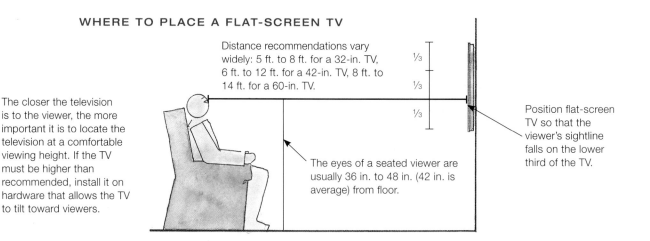

Distance recommendations vary widely: 5 ft. to 8 ft. for a 32-in. TV, 6 ft. to 12 ft. for a 42-in. TV, 8 ft. to 14 ft. for a 60-in. TV.

The closer the television is to the viewer, the more important it is to locate the television at a comfortable viewing height. If the TV must be higher than recommended, install it on hardware that allows the TV to tilt toward viewers.

The eyes of a seated viewer are usually 36 in. to 48 in. (42 in. is average) from floor.

Position flat-screen TV so that the viewer's sightline falls on the lower third of the TV.

more about...

FITTING IN THE TELEVISION

like kitchen appliances, the many models of televisions and other electronic gear often have different ports, configurations, weights, and recommended installation methods. This requires a close look at product manuals and specifications to make sure the electronic equipment will fit into a built-in. Product manuals are often available online, which allows you to research before making a purchase in an overloaded electronics showroom.

A flat-screen television can be static-mounted to a wall or cabinet, and this is a fine choice when the sightline is ideal and the cabinet sides aren't deep. If you plan on viewing the television from different places in the room, or if the television is installed higher than your sightline, consider a tilting or articulating mounting bracket. Such brackets allow you to tilt the TV down to avoid glare or to make for easier viewing (see the drawing on the opposite page for comfortable viewing suggestions) or allow you to pull a TV out from inside a cabinet niche. Check product literature for the range of motion and for any restrictions on the TV's size and weight. Flat-screen televisions are much thinner than tube televisions but they can be hefty, so it's important to make use of any safety restraints that come with the television or on after-market hardware, especially with young children around or in an earthquake-prone zone. Make room for a surge protector or uninterrupted power supply, too.

ABOVE The traditional step-back china cabinet is echoed in this updated sun/media-room cabinetry. A/V equipment fits behind center doors, DVDs are in drawers at left, and home office supplies are to the right, including file drawers and space for a printer.

RIGHT Two walls of built-in bookshelves offer plenty of space for books, art objects, and photos, with enough room for a section reserved for a bottom-mounted television, with electronics cabinets below.

more about...
A TELEVISION OVER A FIREPLACE

ⓘ nstalling a television over a fireplace is one way to keep both the fireplace and the television as the visual center of a living space, but several concerns should be addressed first. Check product literature for your selected model for any recommendations on TV-over-fireplace placement and, of course, to see if placing the TV over a fireplace could void the warranty. In an existing living space, check the temperature of the proposed TV location, taping a thermometer to the wall and building a fire. Let it burn for several hours and check the thermometer. Some experts suggest that if the temperature is 90°F or above, a TV won't survive long over the fireplace. A hefty projecting mantel may reduce the temperature, but soot and smoke can be an issue, too. A television placed over a fireplace with a tall opening or a substantial hearth may be too high for comfortable viewing. A tilting wall mount could help create a better viewing angle. Finally, a masonry chimney will make a TV more difficult to hang and makes it tough to conceal wiring. Some models are designed with frames that look like a painting when the TV is turned off, and some models feature a screen that becomes mirrored, which gives the turned-off TV a more traditional look.

ABOVE In this city apartment, a low fireplace allows the TV to sit low enough for easy viewing. The TV is recessed into a black steel-lined niche, and three speakers are concealed behind a removable black steel-mesh panel. Built-in zebrawood wall cabinets with recessed finger pulls keep A/V equipment, books, and toys neatly out of sight but still within reach.

ABOVE A completely paneled den/sunroom in a new addition is well served by built-in adjustable bookshelves with a niche for a wall-mounted television, placing it at the perfect viewing angle. The drawer contains DVDs.

ABOVE Two walls of built-ins make for a cheery living space. A deep window seat provides a cozy spot for one or two, overflow seating for TV viewing, and can act as a guest bed. A flat-screen TV is wall-mounted with a separate sound bar below.

RIGHT Balance can be a more effective design tool than symmetry when dealing with two elements of equal emotional or visual weight. In this Texas home, the fireplace fits in a rough masonry wall with a chunky wood mantel shelf above and stout concrete hearth bench below. To balance the fireplace, the television sits back on a built-in console in a large, smooth drywall niche.

concealing the television

●●● OUT OF SIGHT, OUT OF MIND IS THE HOPEFUL mantra of homeowners who prefer their televisions behind closed doors. But doors should be easy to open and should keep out of the way when the TV is in use. The standard door of the media cabinet has been the flipper or pocket door, which opens out, then slides in (the pocket door generally slides between the cabinet carcase and another panel, but sometimes you'll hear both terms used for a door that simply opens out and slides back into the cabinet). While pocket and flipper doors can be mighty handy in other rooms, they aren't often chosen for today's television cabinets because they require much more depth than a flat-screen television needs, plus several inches on the sides for hardware. That's why sliding doors have come back into favor for many of today's television cabinets, with two sliding doors that cover the television, and, when slid open, then cover open shelves on each side of the television. Other options are standard hinged doors, folding hinged doors—which reduce the depth of the door when open—or a single sliding door, which can slide in a groove or operate from barn-door hardware.

Folding pocket doors conceal this television when a fire is lit and conversation supplies the entertainment. When the doors fold and are tucked into the cabinet, objects on the shelves above are revealed.

ABOVE A Craftsman-style cherry and tile built-in celebrates the artful compromise between television and fireplace. Openings for TV and firebox are the same size, with the fireplace screen mirroring the folding doors of the television. A raised concrete hearth ties them together and adds extra seating.

BELOW Rectangular patterns recur throughout this modern living room, from rug to bench to fireplace surround and media cabinetry.

ABOVE A botanical Arts-and-Crafts style influenced the hinges and fireplace screen in this North Carolina mountain house. Those ornately hinged oak pocket doors conceal a television. A raised slate hearth makes for a cozy seat.

designing built-ins for electronics

● ● ● TODAY'S FLAT-SCREEN TELEVISIONS ARE, of course, much longer and skinnier than their tube predecessors, so if you try to fit a new TV in an old media cabinet, you'll have to settle for a relatively smaller model—the same width but much shorter. This replacement TV might leave room for a new shelf, or you could take off the doors and repurpose the center portion for display shelves and install a bigger flat-screen TV elsewhere. Rest assured that technology will change, so it's best to design in some wiggle room. Some givens: electronic components will require space for cables and for ventilation. Even wireless components require power cables, and, of course, some components will require Internet connection. And unless you've ditched your CD and DVD collections for purchased downloaded music and online movies, you'll need room for media. Musicians may want to store sheet music in the media cabinet. Oh, and don't forget room for remote controls, unless you've purchased a system with a single remote control that operates everything.

Although TVs have built-in speakers, movie lovers and gamers may prefer to connect the TV to external speakers for surround sound. Front speakers can be built in to cabinetry and so can side and rear speakers. Many audiophiles believe wired speakers are superior to wireless, potentially requiring a more complex built-in design. Unless you feel really comfortable with electronics, it's wise to hire a professional consultant before designing built-ins for home theaters and complicated audio/visual equipment.

This TV niche has enough wiggle room to accommodate a new TV, whenever new technology beckons. Shallow cabinets on each side contain media, and deeper base cabinets contain more electronic components. Speakers are built into the cabinet's frieze.

ABOVE AND RIGHT A fireplace is the centerpiece in this family room, and window seats on each side make cozy inglenooks. Holding down the ends of this wall are two media cabinets containing the television and its attendant gear on the right and audio equipment on the left (photo right). The television is mounted on an articulating arm that allows the TV to be pulled out and turned toward the center of the room.

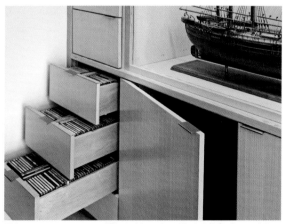

This contemporary maple cabinet is of hybrid design, with frameless carcases but a 1½-in. surround and doors and drawers set in from that surround.

fireplace built-ins

● ● ● THE FIREPLACE MAY HAVE BEEN BUMPED out of the top living-room spot by the television and is rarely necessary for heat, but it's unlikely to disappear from our hearts as a symbol of the comforts of home.

A raised hearth or an inglenook adds built-in coziness to a fireplace, and niches for firewood and fireplace tools are handy additions to a fireplace built-in. The fireplace mantel is the ideal built-in element for expressing the style of your home, whether contemporary, Craftsman, or farmhouse. A deep mantel shelf adds not only beauty but ample display space for treasures that can withstand a sometimes-warm location. Be aware that most codes require clearance between the top and the sides of a firebox opening and any combustible materials. That distance depends on how much the material projects past the firebox.

This new Arts-and-Crafts cherry fireplace mantel is a highlight of this living room. Even when a fire is lit, the mantel shelf is cool enough for what's on display, now Shaker boxes and cut flowers.

ABOVE A one-level T-shaped wing in a small infill house allows for a high ceiling, clerestory windows, and a dramatic focus on fireplace and chimney.

BELOW A rebuilt mantel in an early 19th-century farmhouse gives the fireplace a bit of elegance it didn't have before, with profiled molding. The door at left opens to a masonry chamber meant for warming dishes.

ABOVE Fireplace and television find a traditional harmony in this all-new built-in. The right wing to the cabinetry (a sliver of it shows here) contains open shelves and a base cabinet that matches the left wing.

ABOVE A big screened porch is made even more welcoming by a handsome, elaborately trimmed fireplace with a built-in bench.

RIGHT A wide fireplace and chimney add charm and warmth to this covered deck. The stone-topped raised hearth provides extra seating. A built-in grill to the left is equipped with countertop space for food prep and serving.

gallery

paneling can balance an off-center fireplace

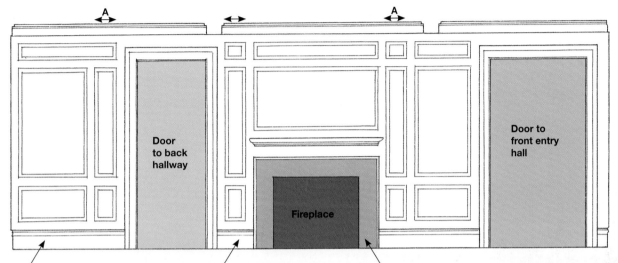

Door to back hallway

Fireplace

Door to front entry hall

This wide panel module is about 8 in. wider than the wide panel at far right, but it appears to be about the same width because of the balanced composition.

The distance between the fireplace and the door to the back hallway determined the width of panel A, which repeats to the right of the fireplace and to the left of the door to the back hallway.

This fireplace (in photo, below) is original to the house and was placed off center between two different-size doors. To give the fireplace a more formal, purposeful look, architect Lynn Hopkins designed new paneling with symmetry around the fireplace and overall balance along the entire wall.

As shown in the drawing above, two panel widths— one narrow, one wide—give the wall composition balance, with narrow panels flanking the fireplace to give it a bit of local symmetry. Another level of symmetry is created by the mirrored wide-plus-narrow panels that flank each door.

built-in shelves for books and display

●●● Along with closed storage for the things you don't want to see, make room for open display space to show off things you do want to see, such as books, family photos, artwork, and favorite collections. Unlike kitchen shelves, living-space displays tend to be less functional and more decorative and are often an exception to the rule that narrower is better. Narrow shelves are ideal for utility—one or two rows of cans or spices allows you to grab and go—but not as ideal for safe and good-looking display of objects, as photos and art objects require a secure home and ample room to show off. Display shelves can be open or covered with glass doors, which not only keep dust to a minimum but tend to give displayed items more importance, a bit like a museum.

Built-in display shelves can blend in visually with the rest of the room if finished with compatible details and colors. Or take the opposite tack with a built-in that stands out as a display object itself, with contrasting color, materials, and detailing. Here's a third option: maintain the room color for built-in sides and fronts and choose a contrasting color for cabinet shelves or interiors. A darker interior can add depth and make light objects pop. For detailed information about shelf design, and for many more shelf photos, see Chapter 2.

LEFT Modern built-in storage and display cabinetry shows off the straight-grained figure of African anigre by contrasting its direction with the horizontal grain on the wide, flat surfaces of the door and cabinet back and the vertical grain on the thick shelves, countertop, and base trim.

RIGHT A living-room entrance is bounded on one side by a dark-stained cabinet that acts both as display and storage. A recessed low-voltage puck light provides sparkle.

ABOVE AND RIGHT These two built-in bookcases are in the same house but on separate floors. The tall bookcase is in a public area upstairs, just outside the bedrooms, and the low bookcase is in the living room. A reveal between the same-color drywall and painted MDF bookcases provides a subtle shadow line. The low bookcase doesn't touch the floor because each case is floating over a slot that opens to a return-air cavity below and behind the bookcase.

ABOVE A clear-stained cherry shelf runs the length of this room. Desk supplies are concealed in drawers, and the double-door cabinet offers a printer-size space.

workspaces

• • •

EVERY HOME NEEDS A WORKSPACE, MAYBE EVEN ONE PER PERSON from school age up. Even if computers aren't entirely ubiquitous in your home, homework may be, and, no doubt, taxes are. Many people work from home, and many more of us are bringing work home from the office. The kitchen or dining room table may handle homework and even taxes, but all of a sudden it's time for dinner, or you've suddenly taken on a big project, and that's when you'll look around for space to tuck a desk or two.

A desk is the centerpiece of a workspace, and count on reserving some of that desk space for computer use, even if a workspace is primarily for artwork or crafts. And leave room for a printer or, more often, a multifunction printer-copier-fax machine. Movable furniture can make for a fine workspace, but built-ins give it permanence and character and can better hide that inevitable tangle of cables and wiring. Shelving is practical even for the smallest workspace, and a multitude of different-size drawers can hide stationery, art, or craft supplies. File drawers are essential for a hardworking workspace. However you set up your workspace, it's critical for health and comfort to design that space to fit the users, especially for anyone using the space full time.

A three-sided painted built-in cabinet is the prime focus of this space. Base cabinet doors conceal computer peripherals and cables, and wall cabinets are filled with open shelves for books, treasures, and colorful supply boxes. Built-in benches offer respite from work and provide space for drawer storage.

configuring built-ins for workspaces

●●● A HARDWORKING OFFICE NEEDS SPACE for peripherals, particularly a printer, whether multifunction or single. A multifunction printer may be bigger, but it handles printing, faxing, and scanning. A wireless model needs only power, so can be located far from the computer, a blessing for your ears if you do a lot of printing. Peripherals can sit on open shelves. Allow sufficient space above for operating the machine and at the sides to clear paper jams. A pull-out shelf in a base cabinet or at waist level in a deep shelving unit may allow better access for both operating and troubleshooting. Full-extension slides are a necessity for any pull-out shelf. Figure out where the door swings when a cabinet is open and the printer is pulled out. A pocket door can tuck into the cabinet, but it requires a few inches extra for hardware, so measure twice and plan accordingly. Bookcases are often deeper than those in a living room in order to handle binders, printing supplies, and even computer peripherals.

LEFT An urban home office has a zebrawood wall that's also the back of floor-to-ceiling cabinets. The wall-height glass door is acid-etched, a technique that makes glass obscure but still translucent, and is somewhat smoother and less likely to show fingerprints than one that's been sandblasted.

BELOW Designed for full-time work, this space has a pull-out keyboard at just the right height, a large display for easy viewing, and a pull-out printer immediately at hand. Cabinet doors tuck into pockets during working hours.

This is one corner of a two-station workspace. A laminate-covered surface for drawing and painting is hinged at the front edge and adjustable for sitting or standing. At left, a cherry cabinet with sculpted pulls holds a copier/printer, fax machine, and office supplies. Tall cherry cabinets at right house art supplies; drawers have low sides for easy access.

ABOVE Built-in cabinets and shelves fill this two-person home office, with the window wall kept clear for plenty of light. The maple cabinet is a hybrid design, with frameless carcases but a 1½-in. surround and doors and drawers with thumb pulls set in from that surround. LEDs light the display case and provide desk task lighting.

LEFT In this home office, frameless walnut cabinets have overlay doors with simple edge pulls. The desk is placed at a low, laptop friendly height, and printer and other office necessities are behind closed doors.

MAKE ROOM FOR CABLES

like any cabinet meant for electronics, cabinets that will house computer components require space for ventilation and cables. Visit online sites or stores that offer desk accessories and cable-management systems. If you have room, install stock cabinets a few inches from the wall to make free space for running cables. Precut holes in drawer and cabinet backs where necessary, and supply one or more grommet holes in the tabletop. Cable-management troughs can keep cables tidy. Another solution for managing cables is to keep cables, plug strips, and UPS (uninterrupted power supply) tucked against the back wall and to conceal them with a removable back panel several inches from the back wall (see drawings below). No matter how many outlets are available below the desk, always provide outlets above the desk, whether in a pop-up plug strip or on the wall. Plug strips are handy for charging small electronics, so make room for several. Look for a strip that allows you to plug in transformers. Some homeowners like to charge small electronics out of sight in a drawer or cubby that's been fit with a plug strip; others like charging stations in plain view.

A REMOVABLE PANEL HIDES CABLES

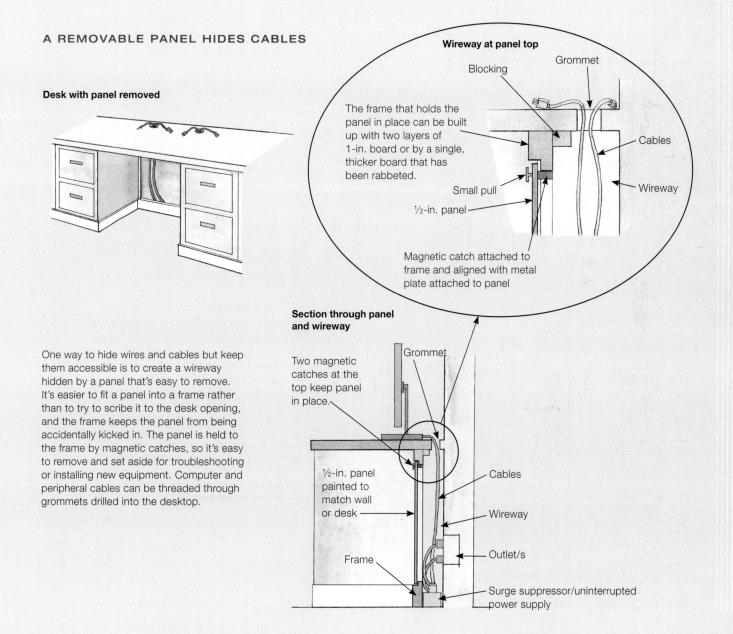

Desk with panel removed

Wireway at panel top

Blocking

Grommet

The frame that holds the panel in place can be built up with two layers of 1-in. board or by a single, thicker board that has been rabbeted.

Cables

Small pull

½-in. panel

Wireway

Magnetic catch attached to frame and aligned with metal plate attached to panel

Section through panel and wireway

One way to hide wires and cables but keep them accessible is to create a wireway hidden by a panel that's easy to remove. It's easier to fit a panel into a frame rather than to try to scribe it to the desk opening, and the frame keeps the panel from being accidentally kicked in. The panel is held to the frame by magnetic catches, so it's easy to remove and set aside for troubleshooting or installing new equipment. Computer and peripheral cables can be threaded through grommets drilled into the desktop.

Grommet

Two magnetic catches at the top keep panel in place.

½-in. panel painted to match wall or desk

Cables

Wireway

Outlet/s

Frame

Surge suppressor/uninterrupted power supply

RIGHT Just deep enough for a comfortable office chair and computer desk, this urban workspace is defined by ceiling-high walnut panels. Recessed metal wall standards with brackets support walnut shelves designed to act as trays with high sides.

FACING PAGE This study is ready for anything. Built-in bookshelves, drawers, and pull-out shelves provide space for office supplies, crafts, and electronic components. A built-in seat allows for a tea break or even a quick nap.

a workspace fits in anywhere

● ● ● A workspace can be barely bigger than a laptop, or it can be a whole room. You can dedicate a corner of a shared space to a workspace or you can carve out space from under a stair or borrow a couple of feet from a wide hallway. If a family member is earning a living working from home, a dedicated workspace is ideal, even if it's not an entire room. Keep part-time workspaces fairly close to kitchen/family/living so no one gets lost online or so a parent can juggle dinner prep with paperwork or monitoring homework. Make a workspace more versatile with comfy seating and bookshelves. Locate workspaces for younger kids—and possibly even older kids—in semi-public spaces like the family room or a large, well-traveled hall so online activity can be monitored. For workspaces in view of public spaces, consider ways to conceal work without having to clear off a work surface in the middle of a project. The best solution is to simply close off a workspace with a pocket or sliding door.

With laptops ubiquitous, an antique desk finds a new lease on life as a workspace.
There's nothing like a comfy window seat to offer respite from work, or, since a laptop
can get around, to even function as a workspace.

TOP LEFT A modest-size workspace has just enough desk space for a laptop perched on a slanted stand, a lamp, a phone, and a few books. When work is done, desk and chair are concealed by a wall-size panel that slides in a track.

LEFT Perfect for keeping an eye on activity both outside and in, this workspace keeps clutter at bay.

ABOVE A space the size of a modest walk-in closet makes a cozy and charming work alcove.

@ workspace that's designed for a full-time freelancer or telecommuter needs to be comfortable for hours, but why not apply proper ergonomics to a workspace meant for casual use? Most desks are too high for comfortable keyboarding, so an attached drawer is essential. It's still possible that the desk will be too high for viewing a screen comfortably, especially for someone wearing bifocals. It's important to keep your head straight or tilted slightly down when looking at a computer screen, especially for long periods. Elbows should be bent at 90 degrees, perhaps slightly more, but not less. A lower desk could help make computer work more comfortable. If the screen is too high, consider an articulating arm that allows a display to tilt in almost any direction. Most standard desks are too high for comfortable laptop use, so if that's your main work tool, aim for a significantly lower desktop or install a pull-out shelf much like a keyboard tray. User size, shape, and eyesight will determine healthy locations. See Resources, p. 166, for a link to a well-researched ergonomics guide.

Building cabinetry with two desk heights so that you can sit, then stand, might be just the thing for an at-home workspace. This works best for laptop users unless you're willing to move the display or purchase two displays. For example, a comfortable working height for a 5-ft. 6-in. person is 25 in. sitting and 40 in. standing. This means a keyboard tray should be just a bit lower than 25 in. so that the surface of the keyboard is at 25 in. It's clear to see that for most of us, working on a laptop requires a desk to be much lower than the standard 29 in. to 30 in. Alternatively, supply the workspace with a comfortable chair that allows the laptop user to work from the lap and still access other workspace amenities, such as file drawers and the printer. Like the TV, a computer screen reflects less if it's at right angles to natural light. Another option is to set the computer against a window so it's easy to look up and out to give your eyes a break.

A simple desk made from a door turns a bedroom niche into a workspace. The desk is attached to the extra-wide cap atop the wainscoting.

ABOVE Built-in shelves and a desk appoint this living/dining space wall for both work and entertainment. Chunky shelves and verticals are functional and sculptural.

BELOW The narrowest of hall nooks is room enough for a laptop desk. Aside from desk height and lighting, what really matters is the presence of power outlets and possibly a jack for wired Internet access.

bedrooms and closets

● ● ●

SURE, THE BEDROOM IS THE DESIGNATED PLACE FOR A BED, BUT IT'S so much more than that. A bedroom contains space for storing clothes and possibly bed linens, and it may be fitted with a TV and audio equipment. The bedroom can be home to a fireplace, a desk for work or leisurely computer use, and display space for art, photos, and books. A built-in window seat is a wonderful addition to any room, but it can become positively therapeutic in a bedroom, especially with a beautiful and private view.

The bed itself can be built-in, with attending built-in headboard, night tables, bookshelves, and storage cabinets, and can be tucked into an intimate alcove with a lowered ceiling. In a child's bedroom, a bed for an older child can be lofted if space is tight, if two kids share the room, or if you want to maximize open space or carve out a bigger homework station.

Of course, built-ins for clothes storage are the primary bedroom built-ins. A walk-in closet or dressing room can keep a bedroom from turning into a dressing room with clothes hung over chairs and even the bed. But reach-in closets can do a fine job for storing clothes if space is designed to fit your needs, with all the rods, shelves, drawers, pegs, and hooks you need. With clothing and linens organized and stored in easy-to-use built-ins, a bedroom can go beyond functional and can become a cozy retreat and a place to unwind and recharge.

Part of a modest addition to a cottage home, this bedroom space was transformed from attic space to a bright master bedroom by two big shed dormers. White-painted built-in base cabinets are tucked under the sloped roof to make storage, with room for books usually tucked into a night-table cabinet.

shaping the bedroom with built-ins

● ● ● BUILT-IN CLOSETS ARE IDEAL FOR MAKING a bedroom more private. Try to locate built-in closets or display cabinetry on interior walls, especially between bedrooms for sound isolation, or between bedroom and hallway. Built-ins not only buffer sound but they can create a sheltered entryway for the bedroom, causing the person entering to experience a change in atmosphere. Built-in cabinets positioned between master bathroom and bedroom make functional sense and can create a visual barrier and sound cushion between bath and bedroom. But it's better for clothes not to be frequently exposed to humidity, so provide a door between clothing storage and a shower or bath space.

Because bedrooms are often on the second floor, a sloped ceiling or kneewall might easily be part of the architecture, but don't let that discourage you from adding built-ins. A kneewall offers depth for carving out space for drawers or shelves. If a sloped ceiling feels oppressive or looks dark, consider adding a shed or gabled dormer to add character and light to the bedroom and to create space for a built-in window seat or a niche for the bed.

ABOVE A chunky freestanding wall gives this built-in bed a sense of enclosure, and it creates a sheltered reading enclave outfitted with desk and bookcase.

BELOW A kneewall in a renovated second-floor bedroom creates a deep wall that's just right for built-in drawers.

ABOVE Attic-level bedrooms share built-in seating with drawer storage.

FACING PAGE Built-in cabinets enhance and enclose separate spaces in this master bedroom suite. In the cozy sitting niche are bookshelves and a tall cabinet that provides privacy.

built-in cabinetry for beds, display, and entertainment

● ● ● OF COURSE, THE BED IS THE CENTER-piece of a bedroom, and there's no reason why the bed can't be built in, too. Building in a bed frame, along with night-table cabinetry, or even a headboard, can give the bed a sense of serenity and comfort. A night table offers space for books, magazines, or an electronic reader, a clock, your phone, a glass of water, and a notepad with pencil for taking note of dream-inspired inventions. Consider creating a charging station in a night-table drawer. A backrest topped by bookcases is ideal for reading in bed or for TV or movie watching. A lowered ceiling over the head of the bed can make the space seem more cozy and intimate. Adjustable light fixtures built into that lowered ceiling, or into a tall headboard, can provide glare-free, one-person reading so that one person can read and the other can sleep. Position each switch to make it easy for either person to turn lights off from bed. And look to the bottom of a built-in bed for storage. Space under the bed is perfect for built-in drawers for out-of-season clothes or linens.

A master bedroom can be fitted with an entertainment center worthy of a living room, with display and book shelves, a fireplace, a flat-screen television, and audio equipment. See Chapter 2 for detailed information about shelves and Chapter 6 for ways to incorporate TVs and fireplaces into a room.

Built-in cabinetry offers storage and display space and helps buffer the master bedroom from the hall.

ABOVE A built-in with display space, TV, audio (behind the center doors), and fireplace promotes this bedroom to living-room status.

BELOW Almost a living room, this bedroom makes it easy to stay put with a built-in niche for a flat-screen TV, a gas fireplace below, and display shelves and cabinets around the corner and beyond.

RIGHT A fireplace adds drama and beauty to a bedroom. This built-in wall with fireplace, bookshelves, and drawers creates a sound buffer between bedrooms.

• built-in beds

The ultimate in built-in beds is the fold-down bed. A fold-down bed can be a space-saving alternative for a studio apartment or for a master bedroom that must also serve as a home office, or it can turn a study or living room into a guest bedroom. You could call it a Murphy bed, but that's a proprietary name for a particular fold-down bed manufacturer; you can also have a fold-down bed custom built by a cabinetmaker—or by you, if you are an intrepid DIYer—that operates with fold-down hardware manufactured by Häfele® or another hardware source.

ABOVE Built-in beds can take up less room than freestanding beds, especially if they aren't standard size.

LEFT This study doubles as a guest room with a camouflaged fold-out bed built into the wall at right. The double bed folds on a long side, so it doesn't project as far into the room as a typical built-in bed.

ABOVE Bed platform and steps to the terrace—with holes in the risers to allow heat to travel—make for matching built-ins. The bed platform is topped with a step for easy access.

LEFT A two-height headboard provides bookcase space above the leaning-back zone and drops down on each side to become a night table with drawers.

RIGHT A fold-down bed turns this urban office into a guest room.

built-ins
for clothes

● ● ● WHAT'S THE BEDROOM BUILT-IN YOU THINK of first? A clothes closet, most likely. The closet is the bedroom's most functional built-in, but it can also shape space and add style. Closets reduce the number of freestanding furniture pieces you need, so they help keep a bedroom uncluttered.

As anyone with an older house knows, the standard 2-ft. reach-in closet is actually fairly new in the history of homebuilding, having taken over from the armoire and trunk. The reach-in closet can work beautifully if it's big enough and properly outfitted with clothes-storing accessories. But burgeoning wardrobes cause many homeowners to wish for bigger closets. A walk-in closet or a bigger dressing-room-size closet can offer space for clothes in a variety of configurations and can corral potential bedroom messiness. One tactic for maximizing space is to eliminate doors, a tactic that works better in a dressing room than in the bedroom itself.

LEFT As compact as ship's quarters but more elegant than most, this master bedroom suite separates dressing from sleeping. Streamlined walnut closets with vertical recessed finger pulls line the hall, a zebrawood floor ties the spaces together, and a *shoji* screen divides them.

RIGHT A serene Japanese aesthetic guides the design of these built-ins, including a shoji window screen and two-tier sliding-door closets, smooth panels at the top, and subtle alternating-grain gridded panels below.

FACING PAGE This handsome built-in closet-plus-window seat is the focal point of a master bedroom.

more about...
SOURCES FOR CLOSET BUILT-INS

C lothes closet storage systems can be custom made or off the shelf. Off-the-shelf closet systems can range from RTI to semi-custom, with parts sized to what you need. Closet storage systems are available in a range of materials. Wire shelving is relatively inexpensive, easy to find, and fairly easy to install. It's great for shoes and hats and boxes, but will transfer grid marks to knits without a sturdy, protective shelf liner. Panel-product shelving (particleboard or MDF either painted or finished with a surface such as melamine—thermally fused is more expensive and more durable than cold-pressed melamine) tends to be more expensive than wire, but looks more traditional and is easier on knits. Closet systems made from mostly solid wood are available and may not be as expensive as you expect. Many manufactured closet systems mount to the wall, which allows for installation over baseboard heating and makes it easy to clean underneath. Several companies offer online or in-store design services for free or for very low fees, and you can have a big part in design decisions. Some systems are designed and installed by the manufacturer and some are delivered to you and installed by a third party, or you, if you're handy.

Closet systems offer a multitude of accessories for every article of clothing you could possibly own. But even if you have an existing closet or plan a custom closet, home-design stores and online closet companies offer an array of after-market accessories that can spice up any built-in closet, manufactured or not.

This built-in cabinetry lines the wall between bedroom and bathroom. Hanging clothes are stored in a dressing room to the right, but this built-in bar makes a handy place to hang clothes while packing for a trip or dressing for an evening out.

SIZING UP A CLOTHES CLOSET

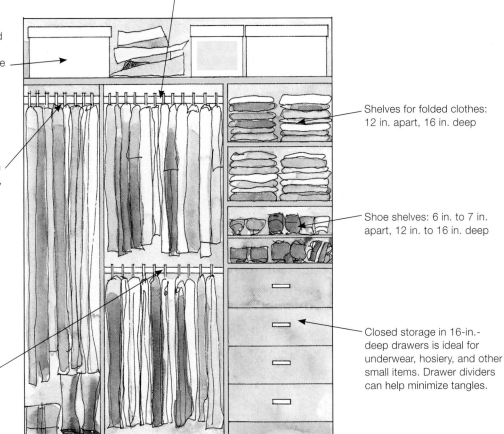

Centerline of upper rod: 40 in. to 42 in. from centerline of lower rod

Top shelf can be ideal for odd-shaped items such as hats and boots and for out-of-season storage. If the closet door is the standard 6-ft. 8-in. height this shelf must be shallow enough to allow you to reach past it to store bulky items.

Rod for dresses and coats can be as low as 66 in. above floor, but raising it higher allows for boot or shoe storage below.

Hanging storage requires a depth of at least 2 ft. Coats may require a 28-in. depth.

42-in. rod height for hanging shirts, skirts, suits, and folded slacks

Shelves for folded clothes: 12 in. apart, 16 in. deep

Shoe shelves: 6 in. to 7 in. apart, 12 in. to 16 in. deep

Closed storage in 16-in.-deep drawers is ideal for underwear, hosiery, and other small items. Drawer dividers can help minimize tangles.

LEFT Baskets can help corral loose items and keep a dressing area neat. Shelves can be easily adjusted to make a space either skinny or tall, depending on the need.

BOTTOM LEFT There's a built-in for everything in this dressing room. Cabinets are wide; a deeper edgeband is applied to the front of each shelf to increase its spanning capacity.

BOTTOM RIGHT Drawers in this dressing room open by handpulls rather than pulls to keep the space streamlined. Shelves divided into cubbies like these are easier to keep neat than wide shelves.

more about...
CLOTHING BUILT-INS

there's a rule of thumb recommending that 75 percent of clothing storage space should be for hanging clothes. But that may not suit everyone in the family. Take a look at how you hang up—or don't hang up—clothes and whether you need more rods, more shelves, more pegs and hooks, and possibly baskets. You certainly will want to include rods for hanging long clothes—dresses, coats, evening wear, and some slacks—and rods that can be hung one over the other for short clothes, such as shirts, skirts, jackets, and slacks folded over pants hangers. A reach-in closet must be 24 in. deep to accommodate hanging clothes.

Folded clothes can fit in drawers but are much easier to see on shelves. Shelves are narrower than the space needed for hanging clothes, so consider placing them on a different wall to save space. Think short shelf spans rather than undivided wide shelves, as adjacent clothing stacks can quickly tumble into disarray if you aren't diligent. Dividers attached or clipped to the shelf can keep stacks from getting jumbled. Cubbies work beautifully to maintain neat stacks, and 12 in. wide is a good start, but measure your own clothes to see what works for you. Keep shelves close together vertically so that stacks aren't too

high. Slightly sloped shelves can make somewhat better use of space than flat shelves, but the space savings may not be worth the trouble. Consider a lip at the edge or a ridge near the heel for slanted shoe shelves.

Drawers are great for storing small items that don't sit neatly folded on a shelf, such as socks, hosiery, underwear, and belts. As a rule, shallow is better—and so are drawer dividers—so that you can see the contents easily, but deeper drawers, even up to 12 in., could be handy for bulky sweaters. Drawer faces that you can see through will help identify what's where; be sure to go for full-extension slides.

Include pegs or hooks for robes, belts, scarves, ties, even work shirts or sporting gear. Ties should ideally be stored flat so that they don't stretch, but there's rarely room for that at home, so give ties breathing room on long pegs so they aren't shoved together. For tight spaces, consider installing hooks and pegs that can fold against the wall until you need to access their contents. Ringing open walls of a dressing room with Shaker pegs can help manage frequently worn clothes, such as bathrobes, along with odd-shaped items, such as hats.

Wide, two-handled drawers in this handsome built-in offer storage space for seasonal linens and clothes.

LEFT A shallow built-in tie cupboard appended to the built-in closet makes it easy to select a tie. The deep cornice wraps the top of the built-in closets, takes a turn at the tie-cupboard bump-out, then caps the window casing.

RIGHT AND BELOW Built-in maple cabinetry fills the entire north wall of this home, with low cabinets at windows and a tall, asymmetrical chest of drawers between. Full-height cabinetry creates a hallway buffer between bedroom and master bath. A pocket door conserves space.

His-and-her dressing alcoves fit between bedroom and bathroom. Closets stay low to make the room feel airy and to take advantage of daylight.

•dressing rooms and walk-in closets

A walk-in closet can corral clothes so they stay in one space instead of getting sprinkled throughout the bedroom. A big walk-in closet—call it a dressing room—allows the activity of dressing to be private—and warmer if the bedroom is kept cool for sleeping. A walk-in closet, and certainly a dressing room, requires a mirror, preferably one that allows you to see from head to toe. Other dressing-room amenities may include an ironing board and iron, possibly electronics such as TV or audio, and potentially a place to plug in a

phone or other electronics. Some couples find morning the only time they have to talk about the day ahead, so the dressing room can become a mini home office.

In a walk-in closet or dressing room, open storage is ideal, as you can always close the door. Some closed (but glazed, for visibility) cabinet doors help cut down on dust, or take a tip from the china pantry on p. 93 in Chapter 5 for shades that keep out dust. Pocket doors are handy if space is tight or simply to avoid a door swing.

LEFT This walk-in closet is outfitted simply, with two hanging rods and a built-in shelf unit, but a chandelier adds a touch of glamour.

ABOVE Vertical-grain fir shows off its fine figure in a built-in dressing-room cabinet. Flat drawers hold jewelry and pocket treasures, and all drawers are fit with oil-rubbed bronze pulls.

LEFT A supremely livable dressing space takes over the top floor of a gable-end addition. Generous built-in drawers conceal clothes while open shelves provide color and shadow.

built-ins for kids' bedrooms

●●● KIDS OFTEN SPEND A LOT MORE TIME IN their bedrooms than adults do in theirs, and built-ins can provide smart storage and create a kid-friendly atmosphere. As a rule, pegs and hooks are better than hangers for kids who are old enough to put away clothes, but a few hangers are necessary for dress clothes, and older kids will require more rod space for their bigger, longer wardrobes. Drawers are handy for small items like socks and underwear, but consider built-in shelves for folded clothes, as kids (adults, too) often graze drawers, skimming off the top 2 in. but never digging to the deeper layers of perfectly clean but hidden clothes. Open shelves can look tangled quickly, so consider fitting lower shelves with lightweight storage baskets or boxes for storing everything from clothes to toys. While built-in shelves are a big help with storing and retrieving clothes and other kid gear, there's nothing more beneficial for maintaining neatness and sanity than built-in doors.

A floor-to-ceiling hutch contains everything from toys to clothes. Doors open with recessed finger pulls for a kid-friendly streamlined look. The desk turns the corner to make a shelf over the boxed-in radiator.

ABOVE A ladder makes a built-in mezzanine playloft and adjoining attic playspace more fun to get to and doesn't take up as much space as a stair.

ABOVE LEFT This two-person bedroom built-in includes two beds, two desks, and plenty of drawer and tack space.

RIGHT A preschooler's bedroom closet is open for the time being (the door can close when teenage clothes start to add—and pile—up). A wall rack keeps favorite books on view.

kids' play and workspaces

Little kids may be small, but they often need lots of space to store toys and games and storage design that encourages putting toys away. This makes built-ins ideal for children's bedrooms and playrooms. Start low and spread out built-ins horizontally so that they can be reached. You may also want to include tall storage that kids can't reach. Although a floor is the ideal play area for most little kids, a kid-size built-in desk can help keep crayons and play clay off the floor.

Built-ins can create order, but they can also create enjoyable spaces and magical nooks and crannies. Older kids require a desk for homework, and they will love built-in display shelves for their treasures and a built-in niche for cozy reading.

ABOVE A column and chase are furred out to make a display bump-out in this city-kids' bedroom. The bump-out is covered with boards to draw or tack to, including magnetic, painted Homasote® , and dry-erase surfaces.

RIGHT A wall of built-in cabinets makes for a cheerful playroom. Shelves with 1½-in.-thick edgeband are fixed, while the thin, ¾-in. shelves are adjustable. Blackboard paint turns the end wall into a giant chalkboard.

ABOVE Window seats do double duty as toy shelves, with base trim cut out to allow for heat from the radiators under the windows. The built-in desk is finished with a solid-surface top.

LEFT The inside of the built-in seat is fit up with partitioned interiors and removable shelves. Cantilevered 1¼-in. shelves are bolted into the brick wall behind the drywall.

bathrooms

● ● ●

BATHROOMS DEPEND ON BUILT-INS FOR CONVENIENCE, DISCRETION, and comfort. A standard list of built-ins for a full-size bathroom will likely include a tub with shower or stand-alone shower, a sink in a vanity cabinet, deep shelf storage for towels and washcloths, shallow shelf storage for toiletries and other small items, a laundry hamper, and cabinet space. You could revise that list to incorporate a separate toilet compartment, a soaking tub, a pedestal sink, a full-height linen closet for both bathroom and bedroom linens, and perhaps even to fit in a washer and dryer.

Smaller additions to the list could be a niche for shampoo and soap built into the shower wall or single shelves for displaying decorative items or potted plants. And don't forget to build in plenty of bars and hooks for towels. Hooks by the shower or bath are great for temporary storage, but they won't allow towels to dry properly the way towel bars do.

Clever built-in design matters far more than size. For example, the deeper shelves designed for towels aren't ideal for toiletries, which are much easier to see and retrieve when they are stored on shallow shelves. An alternative to offering two depths of shelving is to store toiletries on deep shelves but in baskets both to corral small items and allow them to be easy to see and pull out. Fixed shelves can work for towels, but deep-cabinet storage for small items will be better served with pull-out shelves.

Energy efficiency and renewable materials determined the design of this beautiful bathroom, beginning with the wall-hung bamboo cabinetry with quartz countertop.

shaping a bathroom with built-ins

●●● WELL-POSITIONED BUILT-INS CAN ELEVATE a bathroom from utilitarian to a place of tranquility. Cabinets and open shelves offer storage and style, and, if they are positioned right, their mass can help create private zones. Build a full-height storage cabinet near the bathroom door to create a built-in transition from public to private. The primary peace-inducing built-ins are showers and tubs, so make these spacious enough for comfort but protected enough to offer the amount of privacy you desire. A built-in partition for the toilet can help make a big bathroom more comfortable. Two sinks with a shared cabinet between them can ease morning and nighttime bathroom routines for a couple or for kids sharing a bathroom. Built-in niches for storing toiletries and towels and alcoves for bathing or grooming add both utility and charm. Consider universal design suggestions for bathrooms, such as space for a wheelchair, a cantilevered sink, sturdy grab bars at toilet and shower, and pull-out shelves for easier access. See the drawing on p. 151 for guidelines on where to place bathroom built-ins.

Glass and mirrors multiply the effect of built-ins in this cool, blue bathroom.

RIGHT The storage alcove with built-in cabinets consolidates linens in drawers and toiletries and toilet paper on shelves in the cabinet above.

BELOW Shallow open shelves flanking each sink provide space for towels and baskets of toiletries. A door-free built-in shower with a low curb is big enough for two and has hooks for several towels.

more about...
LIGHTING BATHROOM BUILT-INS

good lighting can do wonders for bathroom built-ins. Daylight is a bonus, but not always possible. If a bathroom has no window, or you'd like to build a shower on a wall that's close to the neighbor, look for a way to add a skylight that can spill light on a long wall of the bathroom. As for lighting, be sure to consider the three types: task lighting for safe and easy grooming, ambient lighting for overall comfort and enjoyment, and accent lighting for highlighting textures, collections, or details. At the sink, wall-mounted sconces, vertical lights, or even pendant lights placed close to eye level on each side of the mirror are ideal for task lighting. Overhead lights can work if they don't shine on your face and create shadows. One such option is to install a recessed or shaded warm fluorescent-tube fixture that runs the length of the mirror and that shines on the mirror, not on your face. For ambient lighting, a pendant or surface-mounted light in the center of the room can bounce light off the ceiling and walls.

A tall hutch with glass doors adjoins the vanity cabinet and acts as a visual barrier from the entryway. A custom built-in medicine cabinet spans the vanity with doors over each sink.

more about...

THE TOILET

t he toilet may be a necessary built-in but it's awkward in so many ways, starting with where to put it. Even if space is tight, try to place the toilet so that it isn't the first thing you see when you open the door. For a big and busy bathroom, consider locating the toilet in a separate room, preferably with a small sink—essentially a powder room. A simple, partitioned toilet may work almost as well if bathroom users aren't averse to a lack of privacy. A wall-hung toilet leaves the floor free for easy cleaning, but costs much more than a standard pedestal toilet, and a wall-mount with an in-wall tank requires a thicker-than-standard wall.

The space above the toilet can be prime real estate for storage. A shallow cabinet works well here as do open shelves if that's your fancy. A deeper cabinet can fit higher up on the wall if it clears the head of anyone standing up after using the toilet. Be sure extra toilet paper is stored within reach of the toilet, either in a vanity cabinet or on shelves or in a cabinet above the toilet. Toilet-cleaning supplies can be stored in a closed cabinet nearby.

SIZING UP BATHROOM BUILT-INS

These dimensions are those recommended by the NKBA. Minimum allowable dimensions are often smaller, while dimensions that provide access for limited mobility are often larger. Check the NKBA (see Resources, p. 166) for minimum dimensions and access standards.

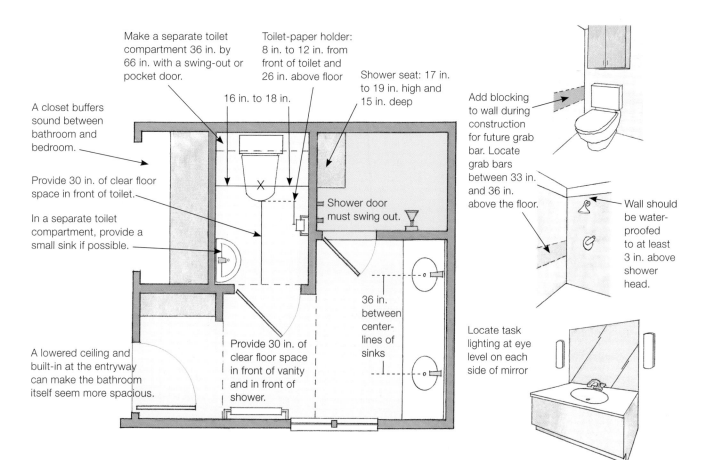

Make a separate toilet compartment 36 in. by 66 in. with a swing-out or pocket door.

Toilet-paper holder: 8 in. to 12 in. from front of toilet and 26 in. above floor

Shower seat: 17 in. to 19 in. high and 15 in. deep

A closet buffers sound between bathroom and bedroom.

16 in. to 18 in.

Provide 30 in. of clear floor space in front of toilet.

In a separate toilet compartment, provide a small sink if possible.

Shower door must swing out.

A lowered ceiling and built-in at the entryway can make the bathroom itself seem more spacious.

Provide 30 in. of clear floor space in front of vanity and in front of shower.

36 in. between center-lines of sinks

Add blocking to wall during construction for future grab bar. Locate grab bars between 33 in. and 36 in. above the floor.

Wall should be water-proofed to at least 3 in. above shower head.

Locate task lighting at eye level on each side of mirror

Thick marble shelves, a matching bench, and equally thick wood shelves give a solid, modern look to this beautiful bathroom. Lighting under the bench adds warmth to the shower room, which has no windows.

more about...
POWDER-ROOM BUILT-INS

ⓛ ocal codes may specify wider clearances, but national standards require the centerline of a toilet to be a minimum of 15 in. from the wall and a clearance of 21 in. between the front of the toilet and the wall. With a 27-in.-deep toilet, this means a 30-in. by 48-in. powder room. That's pretty tight. A more comfortable minimum size is 3 ft. wide and 5 ft. long. There's not much variety in toilet sizes, so look to the lavatory for space saving. A wall-mounted model will free up space, but you'll want to look for storage space, perhaps recessed between studs or in a shallow cabinet mounted over the toilet. Because of its diminutive size, a public-area powder room is a great place to spend a little more on built-in finishes, fittings, hardware, and lighting.

Built-in cabinetry with both solid and glass doors offers storage for bathroom staples and decorative objects and makes a traditional pairing with the freestanding tub.

Mirrors magnify the apparent size of this not-quite-3-ft.-wide powder room, making the most of the ribbon mahogany cabinet and cedar tongue-in-groove ceiling. Cabinet pulls are influenced by Chinese calligraphy, and the floor and walls are limestone.

ABOVE AND LEFT When the need for a mirror over the sink conflicts with the desire for natural light, a hidden window makes a diplomatic compromise.

bathroom cabinets

●●● CABINET BASICS ARE DISCUSSED IN Chapter 2; this chapter offers suggestions for bathroom cabinets in particular. A vanity cabinet is the most common bathroom cabinet. Choose its height based on your height and the sink type. A vessel sink, which sits on top of the countertop, requires a lower countertop than the more common undermount, integral, or drop-in sink. Vanity cabinets are traditionally between 30 in. to 32 in. high, and that could still work well with a vessel sink. A vanity with a standard sink might be more comfortable for tall people at 36 in. high. An off-the-shelf vanity cabinet can be made higher by placing it on a high base, or it can be hung from the wall like a wall cabinet, off the floor completely. Suspending a vanity cabinet requires careful coordination with the plumber early on. Vanity cabinets run from 18 in. to 24 in. deep. Make this choice based on sink size and type and the space available in your bathroom. Consider topping parts of a vanity cabinet with wall cabinets that extend from the countertop to the ceiling or just shy of it, and finish the top with crown molding.

a medicine cabinet isn't a necessity, but shallow shelves for storing small toiletries and grooming supplies are essential. If plumbing pipes aren't directly behind the sink, a medicine cabinet can be recessed in the wall over a vanity sink; otherwise it will have to be surface-mounted, or you can locate it on a nearby wall and place a plain mirror on the wall over the sink. If medicine cabinets really do contain medicines (which actually don't store well in a humid environment), make sure they are high or lockable, or both.

ABOVE A Craftsman-style bathroom features a quartersawn oak cabinet with frame-and-panel doors.

RIGHT Mahogany paneling and cabinetry warms a modest-size vanity corner in a master bathroom. Pendant compact fluorescent fixtures provide energy-efficient task lighting.

FACING PAGE Overlay drawers and doors with discreet thumb pulls keep the design streamlined. High windows add light without compromising privacy.

•outfitting cabinets

Of course, cabinets don't need doors. Simple
cabinet cases with fixed or adjustable shelves
create good-looking storage for towels and can
be especially handy near a shower or tub. Choose
cabinet accessories that can make bathroom
storage tidier and easier to see, such as drawer
dividers for small items, pull-out shelves for base
cabinets, and specialized items such as hampers
and trash bins. While you can purchase accessories
as aftermarket add-ons, make decisions about
hardware early. Knobs and pulls can add style
and color to bathroom cabinetry without breaking
the bank, but you will find it worthwhile in the long
run to specify high-quality full-extension slides for
drawers and pull-out shelves.

RIGHT Painted wood and MDF cabinetry has inset frame-and-panel
doors and flat-slab drawers of varying depths. The beveled-edge
mirror is framed into two sections (the right side opens to reveal a
window (see p. 153, lower right).

BELOW Toiletries are stored in the tall, shallow-wall upper cabinet
and in several shallow drawers. Extra toilet paper and cleaning
supplies are kept under the sink. Open, slatted shelves add a more
casual look of beach-house storage and make it easy to grab a towel.
A pocket door increases the available floor area.

ABOVE Walnut vanity cabinetry makes a deep contrast
to gray walls and marble countertop and backsplash.

A cypress cabinet made from salvaged wood makes a handsome vanity cabinet and recessed medicine cabinet in a Martha's Vineyard house.

sink and vanity

●●● THE BATHROOM SINK, CALLED A LAVATORY in industry jargon, can be showier than its kitchen counterpart because it doesn't undergo as rigorous a workout. Pedestal sinks, which stand alone, can make a small bathroom feel much larger, but they don't offer vanity-cabinet storage. Wall-mounted sinks are ideal for wheelchair access but also require you to create storage elsewhere.

Vessel sinks, which sit atop the cabinet, run the gamut of shape, material, color, and size and can make a big splash style-wise. A vessel sink requires careful coordination between cabinet height and depth and fixture type and location, and it must be positioned properly to make it comfortable to use. Self-rimming sinks are common but not uniform. In fact, they come in a variety of sizes and can fit into any countertop material. Undermount sinks require a monolithic countertop material such as stone, solid surface, composite, or cast concrete because the edge of the countertop is exposed. Stone and concrete must be sealed.

Sink placement depends on who is using the bathroom and when. Two sinks are great for little kids who find it fun to share a space, but teens are keen on privacy, so two sinks may be overkill. A couple with the same morning schedule often share a bathroom with two sinks, but this layout works better if other functions in the bathroom are compartmentalized, with the toilet in its own room and perhaps even the shower. With any sink, consider installing a faucet that can operate with a foot pedal. That way kids—and adults—won't need reminding to turn off the water as they brush and the sink won't overflow because a faucet was left on.

IKEA cabinets and ceramic washbasins make up a master bathroom vanity. The countertop is butcher block. Warm fluorescent lighting runs the length of the mirror to provide task lighting.

ABOVE This bathroom is fitted with a floating wall-mounted bamboo cabinet for ease of cleaning and to maximize efficiency of the radiant heat under the tile floor. Cantilevered shelves are bolted to studs for a streamlined look.

A bathroom with no exterior wall depends on a shallow skylight for plenty of natural light. A half-height wall separates the stock-cabinet vanity cabinet from a bathing alcove.

Teak makes a beautiful wood for these overlay cabinet drawers and shower bench (far right), and it holds up well in the moist atmosphere of the bathroom.

tubs and showers

● ● ● A BATHTUB FITTED WITH A SHOWER IS still a popular bathroom necessity, but many new homes and remodels are looking to a stand-alone shower and sometimes a soaking tub. As a rule, a shower is a much more practical choice, as a soaking tub often gets a fraction of the use that a shower does, especially when little kids are old enough to shower. If you are shopping for a tub to use as both shower and tub, look for a wide, not-too-tall tub with a close-to-flat bottom so that it's easy to step in and to stand while taking a shower. A tub with a flange allows tile or a shower surround to be installed over the flange for a more watertight joint. With or without a flange, with the proper substrate and well-done caulking with a high-quality sealant, a tile surround can make a good shower enclosure. The most waterproof tub/shower container is a one-piece tub enclosure, but these aren't high style and may not fit through a door for a renovation. Sectional enclosures are also available for maneuvering through tight spots.

Unless it's freestanding, a tub that's just a tub still needs attention to waterproofing. Its deck and surrounds can be any kind of tile or can be a stone or solid-surface or composite that's been cut or molded to receive a self-rimming or undermount tub. A wide deck offers space to sit before getting in the tub. Tubs with water jets or other powered features require side access by way of a removable panel or surround. Whatever the tub, provide space close at hand for toiletries and towels. Open shelves or cubbies at the end of the tub or a niche carved into the wall are all practical and attractive built-in storage solutions. Whatever washing fixtures you choose, always provide hooks for a towel and a robe within arm's reach.

LEFT A shower plus soaking tub share space in a low-curbed bathing alcove with a frameless glass surround. A contrast in black, the vanity cabinet has reveal overlay doors and drawers.

RIGHT A hall, a powder room, and a cramped bathroom were combined to make a master bathroom. Mahogany cabinets are fitted with pull-out shelves and a combination of sliding and swinging doors.

The large picture window over a soaking tub has motorized shades for night-time bathing. Big blue-green glass tiles on walls and tub surround add cool comfort in a hot climate. The built-in cabinet at right holds towels and toiletries, and the shelf at left extends to form the vanity top.

shower enclosures

●●● SHOWER-ONLY STALLS CAN BE AS SMALL as 32 in. square, but it's worth it to add just 6 in. to 10 in. to each dimension for a much more comfortable place to shower. This may even allow space for a shower seat. A niche for toiletries rather than a projecting shelf or basket will make the shower more spacious.

How to surround the shower—or a tub/shower—is a critical issue and can impact the shower size. A steam shower requires an enclosure that completely seals off the shower stall. The European-born wet room features a shower with a curtain or screen but no curb. The entire bathroom is built to get either wet or damp during a shower. Toilet paper and towels must be stored behind doors. This can be a great design for an access-friendly bathroom. A more typical shower has a curb with a shower curtain or door at minimum and more glazed panels where not surrounded by solid walls. One-piece and sectional molded shower stalls are available for quick, watertight installation, but you may prefer the style options of tile with a glass enclosure. Glass shower enclosures can be frameless, which better show off shower fittings and wall finishes, or framed, which are generally less expensive and offer a sturdier look. Clear glass is harder to keep clean than frosted or textured. Doors can be swinging (and they must swing out, so look for a style with a gutter if you don't mind the look), folding, or sliding.

This showerhead centered under the skylight creates the sensation of an outdoor rain shower, but warmer. The almost-invisible glass enclosure rolls open on a long rod. Shower benches, frame, and bathroom bench are made from ipe.

ABOVE This sunstruck space is a wet room, with no barrier around the shower, which drains through the grate under the window. The toilet is at right, behind the cabinet with open shelves.

RIGHT A master bathroom is fitted with wall-mounted bamboo cabinetry, a single vessel sink in a quartz countertop, and a tub/ shower enclosed by a curtain instead of glass.

ABOVE Rather than build the shower wall to the ceiling, the half-height wall was topped with a framed shower enclosure that lets in light and makes the bathroom appear larger. Niches for toiletries and occasional flowers not only add charm but create more elbow room while showering.

fitting in laundry and linens

●●● BATHROOM LINENS NEED STORING WITHIN the bathroom, or as close by as possible. If linens are stored in a hallway, supply the bathroom with plenty of towel rods so that spare towels are available. Build in space for dirty clothes in the bathroom with either a chute to the laundry below or a dedicated niche where one or more laundry baskets allow clothes to be tossed in easily. To avoid a trek to the basement, locate laundry built-ins near bathrooms and bedrooms rather than directly in a bathroom, where the two functions can cause schedule conflicts. Provide space to sort, space to fold, rods for hanging shirts just taken from the dryer, a high shelf for laundry supplies, and space to stash a portable ironing board and iron. A built-in ironing board can seem like a neat gimmick, but it restricts the sometimes monotonous task of ironing to just the laundry area.

How to position the washer and dryer depends on available space and the washer configuration. A front-loader washer with the standard front-loader dryer automatically creates folding space on top of the two machines, as long as other items don't accumulate there. Installing a continuous countertop over the machines could make for a more official folding surface. A stacked washer/dryer configuration means you don't have to continually bend down during the drying cycle. This configuration could also allow space for a storage cabinet to one side with a countertop for folding. In a home with small children, you'll want to make sure that any cabinet storing cleaning supplies is lockable. This goes for any place where adult toiletries and medicines are stored.

LEFT AND RIGHT A shared linen closet provides towel storage and backup toiletry storage that's accessible from the hallway. Toiletries are accessible to the bathroom via a door over one of the vanity sinks.

ABOVE AND LEFT This upstairs hallway makes a cheery, convenient laundry space. The base cabinets act as a railing and also provide storage for household linens, and its clear-finished wood top makes an ideal folding station. A rolling cart fits in the gap between washer and dryer, and the decorative rack is operated by a rope that wraps on a wall-mounted cleat.

resources

WEB SITES

apartmenttherapy.com
Not just for apartments, this design blog offers inspiration, advice, and product links for your home, and its several books are packed with home design ideas.

buildinggreen.com
From the statement of purpose: "We are an independent company committed to providing accurate, unbiased, and timely information designed to help building-industry professionals and policy makers improve the environmental performance, and reduce the adverse impacts, of building." Membership is required to read many in-depth articles, but plenty of information, news, and links are free. Membership also includes substantially reduced prices for the respected monthly newsletter *Environmental News* and for *GreenSpec,* a regularly updated book and online clearinghouse for environmentally responsible building materials.

consumerreports.org
There's a fair amount you can read here for free. For example, text about kitchen and bath materials and installation and upkeep is available, as are blogs, product videos, and forums, but only subscribers can view the detailed review charts.

designsponge.com
Grace Bonney's Design Sponge is a hugely popular online design blog, and it's a great place for photos and commentary on home design, from storage to whole houses. Plenty of built-in inspiration here and in her new book.

energystar.gov
EnergyStar is a joint program of the U.S. Environmental Protection Agency and the U.S. Department of Energy with the stated goals of saving money and protecting the environment through energy-efficient products and practices. This easy-to-navigate website is packed with information on how to build and live more efficiently. The program reviews and rates appliances—and whole houses—giving the best performing the designation of EnergyStar. Also look here for information about compact fluorescent lamps and other energy-saving devices.

ergonomics
Just about everything you want to know about how to design around the human body is here: http://ergo.human.cornell.edu/ergoguide.html.

marthastewart.com
A long-time source of beautiful built-in details, DIY tips, product links, and great ideas.

nhab.org
National Association of Home Builders has a helpful consumer resource section.

nkba.org
The National Kitchen and Bath Association offers information for design professionals but also serves consumers tips on kitchen and bath design, and how to find a designer. I suggest a close look at the illustrated "NKBA Kitchen & Bath Planning Guidelines with Access Standards." It's online, it's probably at your library, or you can order it by mail.

readymade.com
The DIY trend drives this website (look at the blog, updated daily, and check out its printed magazine!). You'll find fun and useful ideas for conserving money and resources while indulging your creative side.

shelf design
Find out how much a shelf will sag by plugging its dimensions, material, and potential load into this handy online calculator: www.woodbin.com/calcs/sagulator.htm.

BOOKS

PERIOD BUILT-INS
Calloway, Stephen and Elizabeth Cromley (Eds.), revised and updated by Alan Powers. *The Elements of Style: An Encyclopedia of Domestic Architectural Detail.* New York: Firefly Books, 2005.
This book will always be on my resource list as a bible for historic home design geeks. An excellent, heavily illustrated guide for researching hardware, trim, lighting, flooring, and wallpaper styles for built-ins of all types. This big, expensive, and expansive book is published in England but contains many American styles—look in particular for Victorian and Arts and Crafts.

McAlester, Virginia and Lee. *A Field Guide to American Houses.* New York: Alfred Knopf, 1984.
This 20-plus year-old book is still one of the best guides to American house style. While it's really all about the outside of a house, you will find much that can apply to a period kitchen. Look especially at the many drawings of wood trim profiles and drawings of windows, noting proportions, how panes are divided, and operation type.

DESIGN CONCEPTS
Alexander, Christopher, et al. *A Pattern Language.* New York: Oxford University Press 1977.
This small but portly book is a classic 20th-century design book, but it will always be timeless. It lacks an index, but it is packed with thought-provoking design suggestions for designs of every scale. I always have it at hand. You'll find many patterns that pertain to built-ins, such as p. 198. CLOSETS BETWEEN ROOMS, 201. WAIST-HIGH SHELF, and 203. CHILD CAVES.

HISTORY
Rybcynzski, Witold. *Home: A Short History of an Idea.* New York: Viking Penguin, 1986. Here's another book I could read again and again. Rybcynski writes beautifully about how the house became a place to be comfortable (and built-ins have a big part in that transition to comfort).

TAUNTON PRESS

Books: There's just not room enough to list Taunton design books individually, so visit www.taunton.com/books and click on "home design" to find books with a multitude of built-ins. Your library should be well stocked with Taunton home design books, too.

Magazines: Pick up any issue of *Fine Homebuilding* to find at least one house design article, and don't pass up any of their special issues for in-depth info. In my book, they are required reading. Every fall, look for *Fine Homebuilding's Kitchens and Baths,* an annual review of great projects and the latest information on appliances and materials. Every spring, check the newsstand or the Fine Homebuilding website for the annual *Kitchen and Bath Planning Guide*—a roundup of all the products and materials you need to get started on your new kitchen.

Taunton.com: *Fine Homebuilding* magazine and *Fine Cooking* magazine (for kitchen built-ins) have websites that offer magazine articles for a subscription fee, and they also offer lots of free web extras, such as articles, videos, reviews of new products and discussions about residential building trends. If you are beginning the process of designing or building a house—or even the process of *thinking* about it—I recommend purchasing a monthly or annual (a better deal if you have a long project) subscription to *Fine Homebuilding's* archives online, as you'll get not only all past issues but the latest articles. I've been subscribing to FHB since issue #4, but the first thing I do is go to my FHB online subscription to find an article, then I print it out or pull out the physical magazine to read it. Owning a DVD of all the issues (216 issues, from day one through 2010) is handy, too.

designers

Albertsson Hansen Architecture
Minneapolis, MN
aharchitecture.com

Alloy Workshop
Charlottesville, VA
alloyworkshop.com

Anabel Interiors (Kelly Moseley)
Austin, TX
anabelinteriors.com

Arb Homes & Design, Inc.
Austin, TX
arbhomes.com

Arkin Tilt Architects
Berkeley, CA
arkintilt.com

Baldridge Architects
Austin, TX
baldridge-architects.com

Bonaventura Architects
Brooklyn, NY
lb@bonaventuraachitect.com

Butz + Klug Architecture
Boston, MA
bkarch.com

CAST Architecture
Seattle, WA
castarchitecture.com

Conner & Buck Builders, Ltd.
Bristol, VT
connerandbuck.com

Cushman Design Group
Stowe, VT
cushmandesign.com

CWB Architects
(Coburn Welch Boutin)
Brooklyn, NY
cwbarchitects.com

Elliott & Elliott Architecture
Blue Hill, ME
eena.com

eM/Zed design architecture and planning
Portland, OR
emzeddesign.com

Lisey Good
Good Interiors
Boston, MA
goodinteriors.com

Hatch + Ulland Owen Architects
Austin, TX
hatcharch.com

Lynn Hopkins
Lexington, MA
lhopkinsarch.com

Hutker Architects
Vineyard Haven, MA
hutkerarchitects.com

Inhouse Design Studio
San Francisco, CA
inhousesf.com

The Johnson Partnership
Seattle, WA
tjp.com

Laura Kaehler Architects
80 Greenwich Avenue
Greenwich, CT
laurakaehlerarchitects.com

KitchenLab, LLC (Rebekah Zaveloff)
Chicago, IL
kitchenlab-chicago.com

Jeffrey R. Matz, LLC
Greenwich, CT
jrmallc.com

Dominic Paul Mercandante
Belfast, ME
dpmercandante.com

Lake/Flato Architects
San Antonio, TX
lakeflato.com

Peregrine Design/Build
South Burlington, VT
peregrinedesignbuild.com

Pill Maharam Architects
Shelburne, VT
pillmaharam.com

Pinehills
Plymouth, MA
pinehills.com

Polhemus Savery DaSilva
Chatham, MA
psdab.com

Brad Rabinowitz
Burlington, VT
bradrabinowitzarchitect.com

Rehkamp Larson Architects
Minneapolis, MN
rehkamplarson.com

Miro Rivera Architects
Austin, TX
mirorivera.com

Frank Roop
Boston, MA
frankroop.com

Samsel Architects
Ashville, NC
samselarchitects.com

Shabby Slips Austin
Austin, TX
shabbyslipsaustin.com

Silver Maple Construction
Bristol, VT
silvermapleconstruction.com

South Mountain Company
West Tisbury MA
southmountain.com

Tirmizi Campbell Architecture
New York, NY
Tirmizicampbell.com

Twenty Three 07
Austin, TX
twentythree07.com

Greg Wiedemann Architects
Bethesda, MD
wiedemannarchitects.com

Zero Energy Design
Boston, MA
zeroenergy.com

photo credits

CHAPTER 1

p. 4: Photo © Adan Torres, Design: Albertsson Hansen Architecture, Ltd., Minneapolis, MN

p. 6: Photo © Susan Teare, Design: Connor & Buck Builders, Bristol, VT

p. 7: (top left) Photo © Eric Roth, Design: Dee Silva, Perennial Interiors, Topsfield, MA; (bottom left) Photo © Brian Vanden Brink, Design: Hutker Architects, Falmouth, MA; (right) Photo © Eric Roth, Design: Pill Maharam Architects, Shelburne, VT

p. 8: (left) Photo © Susan Gilmore, Design: Albertsson Hansen Architecture, Ltd., Minneapolis, MN; (right) Photo © Lincoln Barbour, Design: eM/Zed design architecture and planning, Portland, OR

p. 9: (top left) Photo © Stefan Hampden, Courtesy of CAST Architecture, Design: CAST Architecture, Seattle, WA; (top right) Photo © Eric Roth, Design: Frank Roop, Boston, MA; (bottom) Photo © Michael Lee, Design: Zero Energy, Boston, MA

p. 10 (left) Photo © Dana Wheelock, Design: Albertsson Hansen Architecture, Ltd., Minneapolis, MN; (right) Photo © Brian Vanden Brink, Design: Silverio Architecture + Design, Lincolnville, ME

p. 11: (top left) Photo © Durston Saylor, Design: Laura Kaehler Architects, Greenwich, CT; (top right) Photo © Susan Teare, Design: Brad Rabinowitz, Burlington, VT; (bottom) Photo © Eric Roth, Design: Zero Energy, Boston, MA

CHAPTER 2

p. 12: Photo © Dana Wheelock, Design: Albertsson Hansen Architecture, Ltd., Minneapolis, MN, Builder/Millwork: River City Builders & Millwork, Nerstrand, MN

p. 14: (left) Photo © Eric Roth, Design: Pill Maharam Architects, Shelburne, VT; (right) Photo © Susan Teare, Design: Brad Rabinowitz, Burlington, VT

p. 16: (top) Photo © Hulya Kolabas, Design: Bonaventura Architects, Brooklyn, NY; (bottom) Photo © Ryann Ford, Design: Twenty Three 07, Austin, TX

p. 17: Photo © Westphalen Photography, Design: Pill Maharam Architects, Shelburne, VT

p. 18: Photo © Susan Teare, Design: Michael Minadeo & Partners, Essex Junction, VT

p. 19: (top) Photo © Susan Teare, Design: Silver Maple Construction, Bristol, VT; (bottom) Photo © Eric Roth, Design: Lynn Hopkins, Architect, Lexington, MA

p. 20: (top left) Photo © Eric Roth, Design: Lynn Hopkins, Architect, Lexington, MA; (right) Photo © Eric Roth, Design: Howell Custom Building Group, Lawrence, MA

p. 21: Photo © Lincoln Barbour, Design: eM/Zed design architecture & planning, Portland, OR

p. 22: (left) Photo © Edward Caldwell, Design: Arkin Tilt Architects, Berkeley, CA; (right) Photo © Ryann Ford, Design: Miro Rivera Architects, Austin, TX

p. 23: Photo © Ryann Ford, Design: Alter Studio Architects, Austin, TX

p. 24 {top left) Photo © Courtesy of CAST Architecture, Design: CAST Architecture, Seattle, WA; (bottom left) Photo © Eric Roth, Design: Lda Architects, Cambridge, MA; (right) Photo © Hulya Kolabas, Design: cwb Architects, Brooklyn, NY

p. 25: (left) Photo © Ryann Ford, Design: Alter Studio Architects, Austin, TX; (right) Photo © Ryann Ford, Design: Max Hambly, www.cgsdb.com Austin, TX

p. 26: Photo © Hulya Kolabas, Design: Bonaventura Architects, Brooklyn, NY

p. 27: (top) Photo © Eric Roth, Design: Lynn Hopkins, Architect, Lexington, MA; (bottom) Photo © Ryann Ford, Design: Kelly Moseley, Anabel Interiors, Austin, TX

p. 28: (top) Photo © Eric Roth, Design: Lynn Hopkins, Architect, Lexington, MA; (bottom) Photo © Eric Roth, Design: Lynn Hopkins, Architect, Lexington, MA

p. 29: Photo © Hulya Kolabas

p. 30: Photo © David Duncan Livingston, Design: Deborah Lipner, Interior Design; Laura Kaehler Architects, Greenwich, CT

p. 31: (left) Photo © Eric Roth, Design: Lynn Hopkins, Architect, Lexington, MA; (right) Photo © Eric Roth, Design: Lynn Hopkins, Architect, Lexington, MA

p. 32: (top left) Photo © Hulya Kolabas, Design: cwb Architects, Brooklyn, NY; (bottom left) Photo © Ryann Ford, Design: Ryan Street Architects, Austin, TX; (right) Photo © Hulya Kolabas, Design: cwb Architects, Brooklyn, NY

p. 33: Photo © Adan Torres, Design: Albertsson Hansen Architecture, Ltd., Minneapolis, MN

p. 34: Photo © Olson Photographic, LLC, Design: Cugno Architecture, Wilton, CT

p. 35: (top) Photo © Hulya Kolabas, Design: cwb Architects, Brooklyn, NY; (bottom) Photo © Ryann Ford, Design: Hatch+Ulland Owen Architects, Austin, TX

p. 36: (top) Photo © Susan Teare, Design: Peregrine Design/Build, South Burlington, VT; (bottom) Photo © John Wadsworth, Design: Amory Architects, Boston, MA

p. 37: Photo © Lincoln Barbour, Design: eM/Zed design architecture & planning, Portland, OR

CHAPTER 3

p. 38: Photo © Adan Torres, Design: Albertsson Hansen Architecture, Ltd., Minneapolis, MN

p. 40: Photo © Hulya Kolabas, Design: cwb Architects, Brooklyn, NY

p. 41: (top) Photo © Eric Roth, Design: Frank Roop, Boston, MA; (bottom left) Photo © Hulya Kolabas; (bottom right) Photo © Olson Photographic, LLC, Design: Jon Butler Architect, Niantic, CT

p. 42: Photos © Edward Caldwell, Design: Arkin Tilt Architects, Berkeley, CA; Cabinetmakers: Bryan Harris & Greg Tolman, Emeryville, CA

p. 43: Photo © Lincoln Barbour, Design: eM/Zed design architecture & planning, Portland, OR

p. 44: Photo © Courtesy of Howard Miller, Design: The Johnson Partnership, Seattle, WA

p. 45: Photo © Ryann Ford, Design: ARB Homes & Design, Austin, TX

p. 46: Photo © Susan Teare, Design: Jean Terwilliger, Cornwall, VT

p. 47: (left) Photo © Charles Miller, Design: Peter Stoner Architects, Builder/Cabinetry: Steve Mittendorf, Seattle, WA; (top right) Photo © Audrey Hall, Design: Arkin Tilt Architects, Berkeley, CA; (bottom right) Photo © Rob Yagid, Design: JWT Architecture & Planning, Bowen Island, British Columbia

p. 48: Photo © Brian Vanden Brink, Design: Sullivan Conard Architects, Seattle, WA

p. 49: Photo © Susan Teare, Design: Truex Cullins, Burlington, VT

CHAPTER 4

p. 50: Photo © Susan Gilmore, Design: Rehkamp Larson Architects, Minneapolis, MN

p. 52: Photo © Susan Teare, Design: Conner & Buck Builders, Bristol,VT; Mitra Designs, Bristol, VT

p. 53: (top left) Photo © Olson Photographic, LLC, Design: Country Club Homes, Wilton, CT; (bottom left) Photo © Eric Roth, Design: Horst Buchanan Architects, Boston, MA; (right) Photo © Hulya Kolabas: Design: cwb Architects, Brooklyn, NY

p. 54: Photo © Susan Teare, Design: Cushman Design Group, Stowe, VT

p. 55: (top) Photo © Susan Teare, Design: Peregrine Design/Build, South Burlington, VT; (bottom left) Photo © Eric Roth, Design: LDa Architecture & Interiors, Cambridge, MA, Builder: Baypoint Builders Corporation, Newton, MA; (bottom right) Photo © Susan Teare, Design: Cushman Design Group, Stowe, VT

p. 56: Photo © Susan Teare, Design: Cushman Design Group, Stowe, VT

p. 57: (left) Photo © Eric Roth, Design: Trikeenan Tileworks, Keene, NH; (right) Photo © Brian Vanden Brink, Design: Albert, Righter & Tittman Architects, Boston, MA

p. 58: Photo © Mick Hales, Design: Laura Kaehler Architects, Greenwich, CT

p. 59: (top) Photo © Ken Gutmaker, Design: Rehkamp Larson Architects, Minneapolis, MN; (left) Photo © Roe A. Osborn, Design: Larry Crouse, Builder: Graham Contracting, Wayland, MA; (bottom) Photo © Ken Gutmaker, Design: Rehkamp Larson Architects, Minneapolis, MN

p. 60: (left) Photo © Susan Teare, Design: Peregrine Design/Build, South Burlington, VT; (right) Photo © Mick Hales, Design: Laura Kaehler Architects, Greenwich, CT

p. 61: (top left) Photo © Lincoln Barbour, Design: eM/Zed design architecture & planning, Portland, OR; (bottom left) Photo © Brian Vanden Brink, Design: Elliott + Elliott Architecture, Blue Hill, ME; (right) Photo © Lincoln Barbour, Design: eM/Zed design architecture & planning, Portland, OR

p. 62: Photo © Susan Teare, Design: Peregrine Design/Build, South Burlington, VT

p. 63: Photos © Eric Roth, Design: Good Interiors, Boston, MA

p. 64: Photo © Edward Caldwell, Design: Arkin Tilt Architects, Berkeley, CA

p. 65: (top) Photo © Courtesy of CAST Architecture, Design: CAST Architecture, Seattle, WA; (bottom) Photo © Lincoln Barbour, Design: eM/Zed design architecture & planning, Portland, OR

p. 66: Photo © Brian Vanden Brink, Design: Dominic Paul Mercadante, Belfast, ME

p. 67: (top left) Photo © Susan Teare, Design: Joan Heaton Architects, Bristol, VT; (bottom left) Photo © Brian Vanden Brink, Design: Barrett Studio Architects, Boulder, CO; (right) Photo © Ryann Ford, Design: Paul Lamb Architects, Austin, TX

CHAPTER 5

p. 68: Photo © Susan Teare, Design: Gregor Masefield, Studio III Architects, Bristol, VT; Silver Maple Construction, Bristol, VT; Stark Mountain Woodworking, New Haven, VT

p. 70: Photo © Tate Gunnerson, StrangeClosets.com, Design: Rebekah Zaveloff, KitchenLab, Chicago

p. 71: (top left) Photo © Eric Roth; (bottom left) Photo © Eric Roth, Design: Lynn Hopkins, Architect, Lexington, MA; (right) Photo © David Duncan Livingston, Design: Deborah Lipner (Interior Design); Laura Kaehler Architects, Greenwich, CT

p. 72: Photo © Lincoln Barbour, Design: eM/Zed design architecture & planning, Portland, OR

p. 73: (top) Photo © Ryann Ford, Design: Shabby Slips Austin, Austin, TX; (middle and bottom) Photos © Ryann Ford, Design: Hatch + Ulland Owen Architects, Austin, TX

p. 74: Photos © Susan Gilmore, Design: Albertsson Hansen Architecture, Ltd., Minneapolis, MN

p. 75: Photo © Eric Roth, Design: Lynn Hopkins, Architect, Lexington, MA

p. 76: Photo by Todd Crawford, photo courtesy of Samsel Architects, Design: Samsel Architects, Ashville, NC; Dennis Crawford, Cabinetry

p. 77: Photo © Eric Roth, Design: Heartwood Kitchen & Bath, Danvers, MA

p. 79: Photo © Susan Teare, Design: Peregrine Design/Build, South Burlington, VT

p. 80: (left) Photo © Eric Roth, Design: Lynn Hopkins, Architect, Lexington, MA; (right) Photo © Tate Gunnerson, Strangeclosets. com, Design: Rebekah Zaveloff, KitchenLab, Chicago, IL

p. 81: (left) Photo © Hulya Kolabas, Design: Bartels Pagliaro Architects, South Norwalk, CT; (right) Photo © David Duncan Livingston; Design: Deborah Lipner, Interior Design; Laura Kaehler Architects, Greenwich, CT

p. 82: Photo © Westphalen Photography, Design: Pill-Maharam Architects, Shelburne, VT

p. 83: (top) Photo © Ryann Ford, Design: Burton Baldridge Architects, Austin, TX; (bottom left) Photo © Ryann Ford, Design: Lake Flato Architects, San Antonio, TX; (bottom right) Photo © Tim Lee Photography, Design: Laura Kaehler Architects, Greenwich, CT

p. 84: Photo © Ryann Ford, Design: Jim Hejl, weloveaustin.com

p. 85: Photo © Susan Teare, Design: Selin + Selin Architecture, Shelburne, VT

p. 86: Photo © Tate Gunnerson, Strangeclosets.com, Design: Mat & Sue Daly, Renegade Craft Fair, Chicago, IL

p. 87: Photo © Ryann Ford, Design: Miro Rivera Architects, Austin, TX

p. 88: Photos © Olson Photographic, LLC, Design: Jack Rosen Custom Kitchens, Rockville, MD

p. 89: (left) Photo © Mick Hales, Design: Laura Kaehler Architects, Greenwich, CT; (right) Photo © Charles Miller, Design: John Malick & Associates, Emeryville, CA

p. 90: Photo © Ryann Ford, Design: Jim Hejl, weloveaustin.com

p. 91: (top left) Photo © Ryann Ford, Design: Poteet Architects, San Antonio, TX; (top right) Photo © Eric Roth, Design: Lynn Hopkins, Architect, Lexington, MA; (bottom) Photo © Andy Franck, Design: Alloy Worskshop, Charlottesville, VA

p. 92: Photo © Dana Wheelock, Design: Albertsson Hansen Architecture, Ltd., Minneapolis, MN

p. 93: (top) Photo © Hulya Kolabas, Design: Tirmizi Campbell Architecture, New York, NY; (bottom left) Photo © Charles Bickford, Design: Krieger + Associates Architects, Inc., Philadelphia, PA; (bottom right) Photo © Mick Hales, Design: Laura Kaehler Architects, Greenwich, CT

CHAPTER 6

p. 94: Photo © Hulya Kolabas, Design: cwb Architects, Brooklyn, NY

p. 96: Photo © Tate Gunnerson, Strangeclosets.com, Design: John Barnett, jbdenison.com

p. 97: (top left) Photo © Warner Photography; photo courtesy of Samsel Architects, Design: Samsel Architects, Ashville, NC; Creative Woodcrafters, cabinets; Douglas Maderas, fireplace surround; Square Peg Construction, finish carpentry & beams; (top right) Photo © Brian Vanden Brink, Design: Siemasko+Verbridge, Beverly, MA; (bottom) Photo © Ryann Ford, Design: Twenty Three 07, Austin, TX

p. 98: Photo © Durston Saylor, Design: Laura Kaehler Architects, Greenwich, CT

p. 99: (top) Photo © Eric Roth, Design: Pill-Maharam Architects, Shelburne, VT; (bottom left) Photo © Eric Roth, Design: Pinehills, Plymouth, MA; Pinehills.com; (bottom right) Photo © Ryann Ford, Design: Burton Baldridge Architects, Austin, TX

p. 101: (bottom left) Photo © Eric Roth, Design: Lynn Hopkins, Architect, Lexington, MA; (bottom right) Photo © Ryann Ford, Design: Hatch + Ulland Owen Architects, Austin, TX

p. 102: (top) Photo © Hulya Kolabas, Design: Tirmizi Campbell Architecture, New York, NY; (bottom) Photo © Adan Torres, Design: Albertsson Hansen Architecture, Ltd., Minneapolis, MN

p. 103: (top) Photo © Olson Photographic, LLC, Design: Jon Butler Architect, Niantic, CT; (bottom) Photo © Ryann Ford, Design: Joell Ebert, meshinteriordesign.com

p. 104: Photo © Eric Roth, Design: Pinehills. com

p. 105: (top) Photo © David Dietrich Photography; photo courtesy of Samsel Architects, Design: Samsel Architects, TMC Cabinetry (cabinetry), Ashville, NC; (bottom left) Photo © Warner Photography, photo courtesy of Samsel Architects; Design: Samsel Architects, Creative Woodcrafters (cabinetry), Ashville, NC; (bottom right) Photo © Don F. Wong, Design: Rehkamp Larson Architects, Minneapolis, MN

p. 106: Photo © Hulya Kolabas, Design: Stacey Gendelman Designs, Purchase, NY

p. 107: (top and bottom right) Photos © Mick Hales, Design: Laura Kaehler Architects, Greenwich, CT; (bottom left) Photo © Eric Roth, Design: Pill-Maharam Architects, Shelburne, VT

p. 108: Photo © Eric Roth, Design: Lynn Hopkins, Architect, Lexington, MA

p. 109: (left) Photo © Eric Roth, Design: Pinehills, Plymouth, MA, Pinehills.com; (top right) Photo © Charles Bickford, Design: Greg Wiedemann Architects, Bethesda, MD; (bottom right) Photo © Joanne Bouknight, Design: Dale and James Gould, Greenwich, CT, Frances Palmer (vases)

p. 110: (top) Photo © Ryann Ford, Design: ARB Homes & Design, Austin, TX; (bottom) Photo © Tim Lee Photography, Design: Laura Kaehler Architects, Greenwich, CT

p. 111: Photo © Eric Roth, Design: Lynn Hopkins, Architect, Lexington, MA

p. 112: Photos © Mick Hales, Design: Laura Kaehler Architects, Greenwich, CT

p. 113: (top) Photos © Mick Hales, Design: Laura Kaehler Architects, Greenwich, CT; (bottom) Photo © Eric Roth, Design: Lynn Hopkins, Architect, Lexington, MA

CHAPTER 7

p. 114: Photo © Ryann Ford, Design: Jerri Kunz Interior Design, Austin, TX

p. 116: (left) Photo © Hulya Kolabas, Design: Tirmizi Campbell Architecture, New York, NY; (right) Photo © Charles Miller, Design: Inhouse Design Studio, San Francisco, CA

p. 117: Photo © Charles Miller, Design: Inhouse Design Studio, San Francisco, CA

p. 118: (top) Photo © Eric Roth, Design: Pill-Maharam Architects, Shelburne, VT; (bottom) Photo © Hulya Kolabas, Design: Amy Lau, New York, NY, Tyler Hays, BDDW, New York (cabinets)

p. 120: Photo © Olson Photographic, LLC; Design: Wormser Development, Westport, CT

p. 121: Photo © Hulya Kolabas, Design: cwb Architects, Brooklyn, NY

p. 122: Photo © Eric Roth, Design: Tracy Harris Interior Design

p. 123: (top left) Photo © Ryann Ford, Design: Lake Flato Architects, San Antonio, TX; (bottom left) Photo © Eric Roth, Design: Paul Laffey, Belmont, MA; (top right) Photo © Brian Vanden Brink, Design: Dominic Paul Mercadante, Belfast, ME

p. 124: Photo © Susan Teare, Design: Peregrine Design/Build, South Burlington, VT

p. 125: (left) Photo © Emily Gilbert, Design: Beka Walker & Houston Vinson for Shift Design; (right) Photo © Hulya Kolabas

CHAPTER 8

p. 126: Photo © Susan Gilmore, Design: Rehkamp Larson Architects, Minneapolis, MN

p. 128: Photo © Eric Roth, Design: nicholaeff. com, Osterville, MA

p. 129: (top) Photo © Ryan Ford, Design: Dick Clark Architecture, Austin, TX; (bottom left) Photo © Eric Roth, Design: Hutker Architects, Falmouth, MA; (bottom right) Photo © Courtesy of Gregory Schmidt, www. homerestorationinc.com, Design: www. homerestorationinc.com, Minneapolis, MN

p. 130: Photo © Mick Hales, Design: Laura Kaehler Architects, Greenwich, CT

p. 131: (top left) Photo © Brian Vanden Brink, Design: Polhemus Savery Dasilva, Chatham, MA; (top right) Photo © Ryann Ford, Design: ~bel Interiors, Austin, TX; (bottom) Photo ~an Teare, Design: Brad Rabinowitz, ~n, VT

p. 132: (top) Photo © Brian Vanden Brink, Design: South Mountain Company, West Tisbury, MA; (bottom) Photo © Michael Hipple, Design: The Johnson Partnership, Seattle, WA

p. 133: (top) Photo © David Duncan Livingston, Design: Deborah Lipner, Interior Design, Laura Kaehler Architects, Greenwich, CT; (bottom left) Photo © Ryann Ford, Design: Frank Welch & Associates, Dallas, TX; (bottom right) Photo © Hulya Kolabas, Design: cwb Architects, Brooklyn, NY

p. 134: Photo © Brian Vanden Brink, Design: Elliott & Elliott Architecture, Blue Hill, ME

p. 135: (top) Photo © Hulya Kolabas, Design: Tirmizi Campbell Architecture, New York, NY; (bottom) Photo © Brian Vanden Brink, Design: Elliott & Elliott Architecture, Blue Hill, ME

p. 136: Photo © Mich Hales, Design: Laura Kaehler Architects, Greenwich, CT

p. 137: (top) Photo © Eric Roth, Design: Lisey Good, Good Interiors, Boston, MA; (bottom left) Photo © Eric Roth, Design: Howell Custom Building Group, Lawrence, MA; (bottom right) Photo © Eric Roth, Design: Lisey Good, Good Interiors, Boston, MA

p. 138: Photo © Eric Roth, Design: Centerbrook Architects, Centerbrook, CT

p. 139: (top left) Photo © Mick Hales, Design: Laura Kaehler Architects, Greenwich, CT; (top right and bottom) Photos © Westphalen Photography, Design: Pill-Maharam Architects, Shelburne, VT

p. 140: Photo © Susan Teare, Design: Gregor Masefield, Studio III; Silver Maple Construction, Bristol, VT

p. 141: (top left) Photo © Ryann Ford, Design: Shabby Slips Austin, Austin, TX; (bottom left) Photo © Hulya Kolabas, Design: Jeffrey Matz, Old Greenwich, CT; (right) Photo © Eric Roth, Design: Lynn Hopkins, Architect, Lexington, MA

p. 142: Photo © Hulya Kolabas, Design: Tirmizi Campbell Architecture, New York, NY

p. 143: (top left) Photo © Brian Vanden Brink, Design: Polhemus Savery Dasilva, Chatham, MA; (top right) Photo © Brian Pontolilo, Design: Kurt Skrudland, Impact Architecture, Arlington Heights, IL; (bottom right) Photo © Ryann Ford, Design: Shabby Slips Austin, Austin, TX

p. 144: Photos © Hulya Kolabas, Design: cwb Architects, Brooklyn, NY

p. 145: (top) Photo © Hulya Kolabas, Design: cwb Architects, Brooklyn, NY; (bottom) Photo © Hulya Kolabas, Design: Bonaventura Architects, Brooklyn, NY

CHAPTER 9

p. 146: Photo © Eric Roth, Design: Zero Energy Design, Boston, MA

p. 148: Photo © Ryann Ford, Design: Jim Poteet, Poteet Architects, www. poteetarchitects.com

p. 149: (top) Photo © Susan Teare, Design: Silver Maple Construction, Bristol, VT; (bottom) Photo © Susan Teare, Design: Peregrine Design/Build, South Burlington, VT

p. 150: Photo © Hulya Kolabas, Design: cwb Architects, Brooklyn, NY

p. 151: Photo © David Duncan Livingston

p. 152: (left) Photo © Eric Roth, Design: Lynn Hopkins, Architect, Lexington, MA; (right) Photo © Ryann Ford, Design: Suzie Page, Twenty Three 07, Austin, TX

p. 153: Photos © Lincoln Barbour, Design: eM/Zed design architecture & planning, Portland, OR

p. 154: Photo © Ryann Ford, Design: Hatch+Ulland Owen Architects, Austin, TX

p. 155: (top) Photo © Adan Torres, Design: Albertsson Hansen Architecture, Ltd., Minneapolis, MN; (bottom) Photo © Durston Saylor, Design: Laura Kaehler Architects, Greenwich, CT

p. 156: (top) Photo © Lincoln Barbour, Design: eM/Zed design architecture & planning, Portland, OR; (bottom left) Photo © Hulya Kolabas, Design: Rob Granoff Architects, Greenwich, CT; (bottom right) Photo © Hulya Kolabas, Design: cwb Architects, Brooklyn, NY

p. 157: Photo © Brian Vanden Brink, Design: South Mountain Company, West Tisbury, MA

p. 158: Photo © Andy Franck, Design: Alloy Workshop, Charlottesville, VA

p. 159: (left) Photo © Ryann Ford, Design: Anabel Interiors, Austin, TX; (top right) Photo © Michael J. Lee, Design: Zero Energy Design, Boston, MA; (bottom right) Photo © Hulya Kolabas, Design: cwb Architects, Brooklyn, NY

p. 160: (left) Photo © Ryann Ford, Design: Gregory Grammer, Shorelines Interiors, Austin, TX; (right) Photo © Eric Roth, Design: Butz + Klug Architecture, Boston, MA

p. 161: Photo © Ryann Ford, Design: Dick Clark Architecture, Austin, TX

p. 162: Photo © Susan Teare, Design: Silver Maple Construction, Bristol, VT

p. 163: (top left) Photo © Hulya Kolabas, Design: Delson or Sherman Architects, New York, NY; (top right) Photo © James Haefner, Design: Michael Klement, Architectural Resource, Ann Arbor, MI; (bottom) Photo © Eric Roth, Design: Zero Energy Design, Boston, MA

p. 164: Photos © Eric Roth, Design: Lynn Hopkins, Architect, Lexington, MA

p. 165: Photos © Eric Roth, Design: Lynn Hopkins, Architect, Lexington, MA